BOARD SMARTZ

Learning Quips
and
Bulletin Board Tips

Written by
Thena Smith

Edited by
Linda LaTourelle
and
CC Milam

Bluegrass PUBLISHING

www.theultimateword.com
2 7 0 · 2 5 1 · 3 6 0 0

For information write:
Bluegrass Publishing, Inc.
PO Box 634
Mayfield, KY 42066 USA
service@theultimateword.com
www.BluegrassPublishing.com

ISBN: 0-9761925-7-8

1st Edition
Mayfield, KY : Bluegrass Publishing, Inc. 2005

Cover Design: Todd Jones, Tennessee
Proudly printed in the United States of America

Table of Contents

**Dedicated to
my loving Heavenly Father
and to the wonderful family
He sent to me**

Dedication

This has been such a fun book to create for you. My daughter said "Mom, you really are a teacher at heart, aren't you?" I think I am!

One of the first things I remember playing as a little girl, was school. Whether pretending to be a grade school teacher or Sunday School teacher, I was always in the mommy or teacher role. My friends, neighbors, dolls or puppy dogs were my students.

Life happens and it was not to be that I would assume the teacher role for more than a few months, but I loved the time I got to spend in the classroom teaching fifth grade. Those students I taught, are now moms, dads, teachers, businessmen and woman and perhaps, even, grandparents.

They are the cute kids that came up to me on the playground, who linked their arms in mine, and looked up to smile at me. Some are the kids that chipped in together to get me a beautiful robe as a farewell gift, and then there are those kids that wanted a hug or just to have a chat before or after school.

When I visit them in my memory, they are the cute fifth graders who said things like: "Mrs. Smith, you are a nice lady, but you gotta learn to yell!" or "My mom says she doesn't care how Mrs. Smith does things, this is not the way I do it!" "Mrs. Smith, I'm writing you this letter because I didn't have anything else to do."

When I visit this time in my memory, I also see the teachers that I taught with, that had also taught me, in that very school and I see them as the wonderful regular folks that they were and from a grownup point of view. And what fun to realize they were just as nice and just as encouraging as they were when I had been in grade school and under their care.

This book is dedicated to all of you—teachers and my students, favorite bus driver and wonderful principal from that time. I would not be who I am today, without any of you. I love and treasure each one of you.

And of course, this book is dedicated to the family of my childhood, Mom, Dad, Don, Gale and grandparents, as well as, my family today, hubby, Ron, and daughter, Melissa.

And adopted sister, Linda, I didn't forget you! God made me a writer and He sent you to make me a published author. God Bless!

Love,

Trena Smith

Train a child
in the way he
should go, and
when he is old he
will not turn from it.
-Proverbs 22:6

Just a Bit About this Book

When I was teaching, which was only briefly back in the Stone Age, one of my favorite things to do was design the bulletin boards. I enjoyed making them unique and fun-filled. Some of my older ideas might be historically out of date (there have been more presidents now for one thing) but even if the specifics don't apply, the principle idea will.

I know there are different rules as to how much wall space we can use in different states because of fire codes so we want to make the most of the space we are allowed.

I found kids were more interested in the boards if they were included on the board in one way or another. They are like adults and tire of seeing just the top students featured (the 100% kids as I call them.) Find a way to include all of your kids. Everyone has some reason to be featured.

For the first week of school, I concentrated on ice breaking or introduction bulletin boards. There are various ways to include photos of each of the kids in the class. Both the parents and the students love coming to the classroom and seeing that the teacher is already aware of them. What fun to see that she knows, not only their names, but there is a place on the board just waiting for their photo to be added.

As the year progresses each subject and each holiday can be featured as well as each child. One fun thing is to have a student of the week and have them bring a photo and a scrapbook type presentation to put on the board about themselves and about what they like to do.

In this little book. you will find some helps for boards in various subjects. I know that you find many things in other publications. teachers guide books and possibly online but I wanted to share things that exist only in my head.

Bulletin Boards should empower not overpower. They should be interesting and stimulating. but especially for younger students. there should not be so many and such busy ones that they over stimulate or confuse. So have fun with the boards and with all of those wonderful kids no matter what their ages!

If you have a lot of bulletin board space. you may want to cover some of the spaces with soothing colors and change the boards often using the students' work or subjects that appeal to them. You will be able to be freer with your space than the classroom that has one or two boards and no free wall space.

Some of you may prefer to have your bulletin boards bright and inviting and completely finished before the first day of school. while others may want the students to come in and help complete the process.

One suggestion is to prepare borders to go around each of your boards that are in conjunction with the season. Then you will have some uniformity but can use the various boards for different subjects.

Board Smartz

As an avid scrapbooker, I suggest a fun thing to do for each holiday and each historical figure you study that you prepare a scrapbook page from that era or that person's point of view.

For recent historical figures, you should be able to find actual documents, tickets, pamphlets, etc that relate. Around George Washington's birthday, the students can research and create facsimiles. His page could have a journal entry about chopping down the cherry tree, crossing the Delaware, leading troops, life in Mt. Vernon, Washington or whatever the students create. They can use facts, figures and photos downloaded from the web to add to their page.

When studying Geography, the same can be done with photos of the country, and journaling as if the students are on tour there. Different students could be assigned various countries and collect photos and memorabilia to create the scrapbook page either as a hard copy or for the bulletin board.

Another general bulletin board suggestion would be to create a crossword puzzle on the board with the words that the students will be learning in spelling class and using in their language class. Then, work the puzzle with the students.

A Scrabble board and tiles can also be created and for a fun drill each week have the students play scrabble. You can create the tiles as large or small as your board will allow. Another idea would be to create a tic tac toe arrangement on the board and let the students compete by answering questions in the squares.

Let the Fun Begin...

Look for the Key Ideas

🔑 🔑 🔑

Welcome

Welcome Wagon

Welcome to your new classroom.
We hope you like our style.
Come right in and settle down
For we will be here for a while!

I have posted each name on the wall
And will take photos of each one of you.
So that you can learn all of your new friends
Before the week is through!

Today we have posts about people
These are your classmates new.
You don't feel so strange now
As you learn about them and they learn about you.

🔑 If you have a small wagon to place in the front of
the classroom or a cutout of a wagon on the bulletin
board or wall, this poem could be part of your display.

🔑 You could have fill in the blanks posted around
each photo. As a nice introduction, ask each student
their likes: favorite color, food, animal, book, sport and
so on. Be sure and post your picture and favorites, too!

Welcome to your New classroom

Welcome Waggin'

Hello friends! My name is Rover.
We will all be great friends
Before the year is over!
On this board are pictures of us all.
So that we will know
What names to call!

Don't feel bad if you don't know yet
And look up here if you forget!
Your teacher's name is Ms. Cathy
And she is always ready to help you
No matter what you need.
You can ask her questions.
For she wants you to succeed!

Don't you feel better
Now that our names you know?
Once you feel at ease with us
Your confidence will show.
So just relax and enjoy the year
For we are very glad you're here!

🔑 Other ideas would be to have a cutout of a cute puppy dog on the board and the places for each child's photo. The title of the board could then be "WELCOME WAGGIN."

🔑 Be sure to include a photo of the teacher and any teacher assistant. A photo of others in the school such as the principal is a great idea as well.

Making the Grade in Math
Math Vocabulary

Math has its own vocabulary
And I'm learning more each day.
I find it really helpful
To learn more of math this way!

I usually think of English
As the language that I speak.
And always thought that math
Must be a bit like Greek!

But now I find I like it
And I use it every day.
And find it to be useful.
Even in some games I play.

Numbers are a Fright

I really don't like math!
I have to admit.
Each time I start it.
I just want to quit!

I try and I try but.
I can't even sleep at night.
Numbers pop in my head
And give me a fright.

The numbers are confusing
It is all too hard for me.
With all the x's on my paper.
You think my teacher would see!
–by CC Milam

Mental Math

I love to do math.
I do it in my head.
I do it while I'm playing ball
Or resting in my bed.

I love to count the apples
Hanging on the tree.
Then divide them in my mind.
Equally for my pals and me!

If the person at the store
Starts to hand change back to me.
I quickly compute in my mind
Just what the amount should be.

Some folks fear math
And don't think it to be fun.
But of all my subjects
I rate math number one

Do You Speak Math?

I have learned so much about math
And its vocabulary is so fine
That I can't get it out of my head
And it is starting to fill my mind!
I've divided all of my worries
By multiplying my buddies
And I've added a new interest
Which has helped me in my studies!
Sometimes when I'm out walking
I meet someone in my path
And when I say, "Good Morning."
I fear I'm speaking to them in Math!

Pizza Puzzle

Below is a pizza
That Melody wants to share
She wants five equal pieces
Because she must be fair.

But Susan left the party
After five slices were cut
This left them in a pickle
With this puzzle that is tough.

So how can Melody divide it
In the simplest way.
So that all her friends are happy
As they visit her today?

🔑 The pizza is easy for students to visualize and they see this is practical math that they will use. Translate this into circles, round tables and cakes by setting up a display that is in a circular shape. Talk about circular graphs for older students.

🔑 Pizza is not the only thing I've found that is round! What other round things might you have to divide equally?

**Math helps me measure accurately
Things that I need to know
Length, Width, Depth and Mass
As my progress soon will show.**

Is Pizza a Problem?

When you eat a pizza–
In case you didn't know it,
You are in the midst of math
And I have evidence to show it!
The pizza has a circular shape
With measurements we must learn,
And is bought with money
Measured in dollars we must earn.
We must learn how to share it–
Do we divide or multiply it,
And what percent of tip do we give
To the ones who will supply it?
Yes, it is a fact
That before you even taste it,
You are in the middle of math
A great adventure, so don't waste it!

🔑 Most kids of any age love pizza and you can get their attention by putting a drawing of a big pizza on the wall or bulletin board. Get a fresh pizza box from a local Pizzeria and bring it into class filled with circles for the kids to use to figure out the various problems you give them.

🔑 Have the kids take turns pretending to be the Pizza server and decide how to cut the pizza. You can also do this exercise on the chalk board or white board.

🔑 The board can also be filled with various size and color of numbers, fractions, decimal points, division signs, addition signs, etc.

Mastering Math

If you want to succeed
You will need to master math.
Here are some helpful hints
To help you in that task!

Listen for and learn the concepts
Instead of just memorizing how it's done.
Once you understand the whys.
You will find that math is fun.

Listen to your teacher
And facts of math you'll learn.
So that before you know it
Highest marks you'll earn.

Write those numbers neatly
And keep them all aligned.
And you will find that math is fun
And greatly improves your mind.

Masters of Mathematics

Hear ye! Hear ye! All of you who love math.
And find it so exciting!
I hope you will help those of us
Who don't find it to be inviting!

We would welcome your expertise
In helping us get ahead
For some of us just don't get it
And face each math class with dread!

Math Can't Hurt

Students I hear you—
I hear you every day
As you make your frantic pleas
That mathematics would go away.

You say you liked addition.
And subtraction was just fine.
Multiplication is almost bearable
But division blows your mind.

You say that you dread high school
Because Algebra looms ahead.
and you have nightmares about Geometry
While sleeping in your bed.

Don't let math intimidate you
Or cause you to feel sad.
For once you understand it
Math really isn't bad.

Now that I've had my say
And my thoughts I've said
I must add that math can't hurt you—
That is only in your head!

🔑 Below are some samples of exercises you can do
To make mathematics a little more interesting for you!

🔑 Examples could be to show multiplication and division
are inverse operations—and each can "undo" the other.
Division won't seem quite so scary anymore!

More About Math

Keep your numbers neat and tidy
And keep your rows all straight
And if you follow this one rule
You will find the results are great!

Below are some great papers
That followed this rule to a "T"
And if you look at them
You will see grades of A's and B's!

Numbers

I love numbers.
I love the way they look.
I love to write them neatly
In my brand new math notebook!

I keep my rows all tidy
And I line them up just so.
So that as I add them.
Their sum I will quickly know!

Addition and subtraction
Are like music to my ears.
I can't wait until Algebra.
And thoughts of Geometry
Causes me no fears!

Math is for Me!

More Numbers

I thought I had learned my numbers
When I was very young.
I thought I knew everything about them
But boy was I wrong.

Soon we learned of fractions
Of what a decimal was.
And then we learned stuff to do with them
That caused my brain to buzz.

I heard someone mention integers
And square roots and words so foreign
That even though it puzzles me
I know that numbers won't be boring!

Let's play a game with numbers
Let's play a game with math
Let's play a game with fractions
Let's divide things in half!

Let's learn how to multiply
Let's learn how to divide
Let's take a round pie circle
Let's find the number of pieces inside!

I'm learning every day
How to chase
The fear of math away!

Practical Math

Can you list some common ways
That you use math skills each day?
You may be surprised
At how many are right before your eyes!

Do you divide your Halloween candy
As you receive your treats
Between you and your siblings
To make sure you have equal things to eat?

Do you help plant flowers
In rows that must be spaced just so.
With a certain measure of space between
To help them have room to grow?

Then you are using math
When you didn't think you would do it
And as you use it more and more
You will get more accustomed to it.

So count the ways you use it
As you go about your days
And you will find you are relying on it
In so many different ways!

Math is exciting!
Math is fun.
There's something in it
for everyone!

🔑 (Then you can list some examples)

Mary's Birthday Money

Mary got ten dollars in birthday money
And John got a three dollar rebate check.
Sue found a dollar on the street
And Bob picked up a quarter from the deck.
What part of one of these is the other,
How can we figure what percentage to show?
When you develop your math skills,
Soon these things you will know.

Gozinta

I learned a secret
About math today
And I created a game
That I like to play.
I choose a random number
And then I choose another
And figure out how many times
One gozinta the other!

Many students fear math and they don't know that they use it everyday in a variety of ways. Ordering pizza, buying treats at the food court or drive through, and spending their allowance. Help them to discover the usual and unusual ways that math is a part of their lives each day. Discuss the reasons for their fears. Then try to figure out how to make math easier to understand and more fun, too. If you start young you'll prevent that fear from ever forming.

**I will not be afraid of math...
I will not be afraid...
I will not!**

Friendly Math

Math is friendly
Math is kind
Math is certainly
A friend of mine!

It helps me find locations
Of where I want to go
And helps me divide and share
With people that I know.

It helps me find channels
On the television set
And if I work hard at it
I'm sure an "A", I'll get!

No matter what your friends may say
You will use Math most every day!
Some use it at work and some at play!

I know how to estimate
Using what I've been taught
And this is very convenient
To figure sales tax on things I've bought!

2 Good

+ 2 Be

4 Gotten

Succeeding in Science

🗝 A dark background material on the wall or the bulletin board can be filled in with either the solar system or various constellations. As you study various planets have the students decide where they go on the board and add them.

Constellations

Do you know the constellations?
That are above you in the sky?
Do you know which one is brightest?
And can you tell me why?

Their names we've taken from them
To name the days of our week
So you are speaking of constellations
When of your calendar you speak.

🗝 What is the solar system? What are planets? What is the earth? Are we a planet or a star? Do we rotate? What is an axis? Can you name the constellations?

Oh, My Stars!

I bought a galaxy today.
It came in a little box.
Which was filled with stars that glow.
I really like it lots!
I can arrange the stars
In a constellation that I love.
Place them upon my ceiling
To shine down on me from above!

Looking Back in Time

Look up above you in the night
And catch a glimpse of twinkling light.
Do you realize that as you look at the sky
You are looking back in history
As that little star you see?

That star may have started long ago—
Not that its journey is so slow—
But that it comes from so far away.
The twinkling light that arrives today.

Do you know why stars twinkle or
Why they have the colors that we see?
Let's study about the stars above us
And see what the most distant star might be.
Twinkle, twinkle, little star
What a ball of gas you are!

🔑 The twinkle is said to be the light traveling from the star and being bent and twisted in its long trip through layers and layers of gas particles in the atmosphere back to your eye.

🔑 Purchase the glow in the dark stars and have students arrange them in various constellations either on the bulletin board, or if convenient, around the walls. If the room can be made dark enough, this will be a great visual aid and just downright fun!

Unlocking Secrets With Science

Welcome to my world–
A world I love to share.
I want to unlock secrets
That are around you everywhere.

Look up at the sky above
Is it blue or gray?
What is the secret to its color
On any given day?

What about the rainbow.
Are the colors always the same?
What about the length of it.
And the way the layers are arranged?

What are the seasons of the year?
Are they all equally created?
And are some more desirable.
And more appreciated?

Why do leaves change colors?
Why don't pine trees do the same?
How many kinds of plants are there.
And what is a scientific name?

Where did the ocean come from?
And what are the reasons why.
When I glance off into the distance.
It seems to melt into the sky?

Oh, there is mystery all around you
If you just stop and look.
And some of them are at your fingertips
In your brand new science book!

Reasons for Seasons

The seasons are created by
The amount of solar radiation received.
This affects the climate
And causes changes in trees and leaves.

The earth is tilted and revolves around the sun
So that there is a great variety
In the climates of the world
And when our summer and winter might be!

The climates remain fairly constant
As far as patterns in temperature.
So don't worry that sunny beaches will freeze
Of that you may be sure!

The Seasons

Look at what I've found!
A Fall tree looks like an arm of brown
Connected to a hand like mine
With fingers as the branches bold
That the colorful leaves of Fall can hold.

🔑 For younger students, illustrate with the child's arm as a trunk and hand as branches with colorful leaves attached.

🔑 For older students, illustrate with a larger drawing of a tree with falling leaves of red, yellow and brown. Draw a large leaf and label the parts of the branches as well as adding labels to the parts of the trunk and roots.

I Love Fall!

I love the seasons!
I love them all.
But my favorite season
Has to be FALL!

I love the trees so bright
With colors of orange and brown.
And how very pretty the leaves look
When scattered on the ground!

I love to rake them all in a pile
And then jump in them for a while.
Then I lay down on the ground.
And gather the leaves all around.

Could anything be more fun than to play
In the beautiful colorful leaves all day?
That is why my favorite season of all
Should be. could be. HAS TO BE FALL!!

🔑 After reading the Fall poems, discuss what
happens to the leaves and trees that make the
difference in colors and why do the leaves fall in Fall?

**Fall will be fun
But it won't last long
For winter will come
And all of the pretty leaves
Will be gone!**

Feel the Fall

Do you hear it?
Can you hear the call?
It's the end of Summer
And the beginning of Fall!
Can you feel it?
Can you feel the chill in the air?
Unpack your sweaters
And let down your hair!

Fall

Listen carefully and you can hear
The gentle whisper of leaves
Falling ever so softly
To the ground.

I can hear the silence
I can feel the calm
But most of all.
I love the quietness of Fall

🗝 Does everyone have a Fall?

🗝 What is Chlorophyll and what is its role in Autumn?

🗝 What happens to the leaves to make them so easily blown away by the wind?

🗝 How do temperature. light. and water supply have an influence on the degree and the duration of Fall color.

Fall Aboard!

Summer is done!
Winter is on the way.
But that's no reason
To sit and fret...
We still have time to play!
Fall aboard!
And let's jump
In the leaves
And skate on the
Sidewalks until
Fall disappears
And Winter appears
And the sound of
Our skates is stilled!

Summer Fun

Summer fun and Summer sun.
Summer breezes and doing what pleases.
Summer clothes and Summer shoes.
Farewell blahs and Winter blues!
Summer. hurry and come to stay...
Oh. how I love a Summer day!
Lazy. hazy Summer day!
Come and take my cares away!
I'm tired of work
And want to play!

🔑 Is Summer hot everywhere in the world?

🔑 Does Summer have the same length?

Winter is Wonderful

Winter is wonderful
No matter where you live!
Summer has come and gone
With all it has to give!

Fall has slipped away
And Winter is here at last
With sweaters and turtlenecks
It passes all too fast!

I love the smell of Winter
And fireplaces burning bright
With logs piled up inside
Shedding Winter light!

From Alaska to Florida,
In Idaho or on California's shore,
Winter is so delightful,
Each year I love it more!

What is winter like where you live—
Do you have snow and ice?
Or are you near balmy beaches
Where the weather is sunny and nice?
It's nice that there is a variety
So some folks can surf and others ski!

Oh, Winter Wonderland!

Winter is Wonderful

(Kid Version)

Winter is fun
I love it a bunch!
We have hot soup
For dinner or lunch!

Fall was a bummer
For it meant back to school!
Although sometimes it's not so bad,
Some parts are fairly cool!

Winter in our house smells nice
When in our fireplace we build a fire.
I love the look of frost on the windows
When we drive in the car.

Hot chocolate with marshmallows
Crowded up on the top
And 'smores cooked in our fireplace
On my list are tops!

I love it when it snows
Summer has nothing so much fun as that
I love to build a snowman
To dress in Dad's old ties and hat!

Winter can be an exciting season
With lots of neat things to do!
And most of all I love the fact
That I share my winter with you!

We can build a snowman...

Science Fair

If you have a scientific discovery
Or an idea that just might be
Something unique and startling
It could change our history!

Get your ideas together
And sketch out your plan
To see if the ideas you have
On their own scientific feet can stand.

Is there a problem that perplexes you
That you think you could address
By some scientific method
Could you do some project best?

Does the price of gasoline at the pump
Inspire you to find a fuel
To warm us in the winter
And in the summer keep us cool?

Do you know a way to run our cars
Or a better way for us to sleep
With a soothing bedtime relaxer
Instead of having to count sheep?

Does the smearing of the lipstick
Or the cost of printer ink
Get your creative juices flowing
And cause your mind to think?

Do you wonder about water pressure
Or the the effects of velocity
On boats out in the water
Or the ships out on the sea?

continued...

...continued from previous page

Are you interested in erosion
And the effects of fluid flow
Is there a project in you
To show others what you know?

Do you know a way we could influence
How rain and snow shape our countryside
Would you be able to demonstrate the principles
With confidence and pride?

Or are you worried about endangered species
And would you love to watch animals in the wild
Tracking them and studying them
Taking notes and photos all the while?

There are so many exciting things
For a Science Fair entrant to do—
We just furnish the opportunity
And the rest is up to you!

On My Way to the Fair

I'm on the way
To the Science Fair
All of my teachers
And friends will be there.
There will be experiments
And inventions galore
That after all.
Is what a Science Fair is for!

Create a special bulletin board to create interest in
science fairs and projects. Have the students suggest
topics that you can list as possibilities for science projects.

Time to Rhyme!

🔑 There are so many wonderful possibilities for bulletin boards for language skills. For composition boards, you can have famous authors such as Shakespeare for older students or stacks of books with various titles with which students would be familiar.

Let's Write!

Let's write a story!
Let's rhyme a rhyme!
Let's create a drama
And perform it sometime.!

Let's write a riddle-
Or let's all rehearse
What we want to say
In a thank you verse!

Let's write a song
About a holiday.
And put all of this together
In a happy classroom play!

Let's read the classics.
Let's write a mystery.
Once we get started
You'll see what fun
English can be!

Let's rhyme a rhyme!

Create a Rhyme

Finish these sentences
And create a rhyme.
You will catch on
In a very short time:

I love the Summer
That shines so brightly
And I think to myself
???????

Roses are red
Violets are blue
I made a new friend
???????

Today I saw a puppy
Running down the walk.
I watched him for awhile
And to myself I thought.
Silly little puppy
You are going the wrong way.
I'd better take you home
???????

Now that you have gotten started
And see just how easy it can be
Keep on writing verses
How about one of a tree?

Specifically Spelling

Write a list of frequently misspelled words and print each one on a piece of cardstock or poster board large enough to be seen easily from the students' seats. Place them on the wall or board and have the students replace them with a correctly spelled word. Add words to the board from the daily papers.

Spelling Champs

Below are the papers
Of those who can spell
The most difficult words
And can do it well!

Great job on these papers!
I am posting each one
So they can be admired
For the great work you have done!

When I Spell

I learned that when I see the word,
I get a picture in my mind.
Then I think the word
And I can feel the word.
So I say the word and it is mine!

Spill Chick...Splel Cehck... Spell Check!

Can You Spell?

I want to spell correctly?
I want to know my words are right.
I wish I could spell difficult words
To show that I am very bright.

Spelling Bee

We're going to have a spelling bee
And we will soon find out
Who knows how to spell the best
And we'll know without a doubt.
So take home your spelling books
And study them thoroughly
So that you will be prepared
For our spelling bee!

🔑 Place bees and flowers on the bulletin board.
On each flower, place spelling words. For the
Spelling Bee, place the student's name on the bees.
At the end, you will have the "Top" or "Queen" bee.

This little verse was helpful to me
In remembering that in spelling
It is usually 'i' before 'e.'

"I" before "E"
Except after "C."
Or when pronounced "ay" [/ei/]
As in "neighbor" and "weigh."

Getting into Geography

Looking at Maps

I love to look at maps
And hear the names so strange
Of cities, towns, countries
Of rivers or mountain range.

I love to unfold a great big map
And globes I love to twirl.
I guess I just love it all—
The great big old world!

Geography

Hills and valleys
Mountains and plains
Vast oceans and sandy shores
Or fields of ripe grain.
Snow falling on mountain tops
Pelicans gliding out to sea
Look at the variety
The earth offers me!

🔑 Have students take photos from airplanes as they travel or from mountains or tall buildings that allow them to get a different view of the land we live on.

🔑 Create a Geopoly game for the students to play.

🔑 Also check out the chapter on Learning from the Simple Things. You will find more about Geography. the continents. etc.

What Do You Know About...

What do you know about the United States?
What facts can you share?
We will gather them together
So that we can all enjoy and share.

Below are drawings of the United States map,
All done with flair and style.
We are going to learn each state by its location,
And that might take us awhile.

We will start with the Northwestern states
And work our way to the Eastern shore.
And by the time the year is done,
You will not wonder what their names are anymore!

Do you know all the states?
Let's draw a map to share.
Can you recognize them by their shapes?
Do you know how many are there?

How Well Do You Know Your State?

🔑 Suggest the students try to draw their state without looking at a map. Then have a map on the board on slide screen that they can get a good look at and then try to draw it again. Some states (those most square and rectangular in shape) with be far too easy. In this case, have them draw their state and the adjoining state.

🔑 From this exercise, branch out into drawing their regions, rivers, mountain ranges, etc.

List of the States

(Learn in a week)

Monday, we had to learn the states
But the only ones I could say,
Were Alabama, Alaska, Arkansas and Arizona
Because they all started with "A"

Four states that start with "A,"
But none that start with "B."
California, Colorado and Connecticut
Start with "C" while only Delaware is a "D."

Tuesday, Teacher taught us some more
And I know the first ten—WOW!
For by remembering Florida and Georgia,
I'm up to the "H's" and Hawaii now.

Idaho and Illinois
Indiana and Iowa are the "I's."
That Kansas and Kentucky are the only "K's"
And took me by surprise.

Louisiana is the only "L,"
While the "M's" have 8 in all.
Maine, Maryland, Massachusetts, Michigan, Minnesota,
Mississippi, Missouri and Montana...if I recall!

Whew! By Wednesday, I had learned so many
That the "N's" seemed easy to list.
Nebraska, Nevada, New Hampshire, New Jersey,
New Mexico, New York, North Carolina
And North Dakota, almost ready for my test!

On Thursday, I learned Ohio and Oklahoma
Whoops! Oregon has an "O," as well.
Pennsylvania is the only "P"
Oh, I'm doing this so well!

Rhode Island is a tiny state
And the only "R"
But there are two "S's"
If I can just remember what they are!

South Carolina and South Dakota,
Oh, those were easy for me.
And I know there are two "T's"
Texas and Tennessee.

Friday taught me that Utah is the only "U"
But look—there are two "V's,"
Vermont and Virginia
As you can plainly see.

Well, the last ones on my list,
Which seems so very long,
Are Washington, Wisconsin and Wyoming,
I remembered all along!
Oops! Add West Virginia
Or you will have it all wrong!

WOW! I am so impressed
With what I've learned.
I hope Teacher agrees
That a great big "A" I've earned!!!

Look at you,

You've made me proud
Can you say theses states out loud?

🔑 Or maybe you can learn better from a list...

Alabama	Nebraska
Alaska	Nevada
Arizona	New Hampshire
Arkansas	New Jersey
California	New Mexico
Colorado	New York
Connecticut	North Carolina
Delaware	North Dakota
Florida	Ohio
Georgia	Oklahoma
Hawaii	Oregon
Idaho	Pennsylvania
Illinois	Missouri
Indiana	Rhode Island
Iowa	South Carolina
Kansas	South Dakota
Kentucky	Tennessee
Louisiana	Texas
Maine	Utah
Maryland	Vermont
Massachusetts	Virginia
Michigan	Washington
Minnesota	West Virginia
Mississippi	Wisconsin
Montana	Wyoming

🔑 List the states on the wall and have students each choose a state to draw and place beside its name on the list. Identifying the shape with the name will help them when they start to list the state on the map.

🔑 On the bulletin board should be a US map large enough to label states and capitals easily.

Capitals

We learned the states in alphabetical order
From ALABAMA (A) to (W) WASHINGTON.
And now learning their capitals
Should be lots of fun!

ALABAMA, the first A state
Has **Montgomery** as its capital.
And I think everyone wants to go
To see ALASKA, that lovely state,
With its capital of **Juneau**!

Let's go to sunny ARIZONA
With a capital of **Phoenix**,
One of the prettiest deserts we saw.
Then off to **Little Rock**,
Capital of ARKANSAS!

If you like CALIFORNIA,
To its capital you should go.
For it is bright and balmy,
In its capital of **Sacramento**!

I know that COLORADO is lovely
With such pure, clean air.
And I think that **Denver**, Colorado
Had lots of neat things to share!

CONNECTICUT has Hartford,
While Dover belongs to DELAWARE.
And Tallahassee is the capital of FLORIDA.
And I know Atlanta is in GEORGIA.
...Yes, that's where!

Hula girls in Honolulu
Are in the capital of HAWAII.
While the noisy tend to go to Boise,
The beautiful capital of IDAHO.

If you go to Springfield in ILLINOIS,
Their capital you have learned.
And a trip to INDIANA with
Capital Indianapolis you have earned!

Off to IOWA, we'll be soaring
And its capital of Des Moines.
We will find fun things to do-
I know it won't be boring!

KANSAS is a beautiful state
And its capital Topeka is our destination.
And then, to Frankfort, KENTUCKY
Without a moment's hesitation.

How's the weather in LOUISIANA?
Well that's where we'll go.
And I doubt if in its Baton Rouge capital
We run the risk of snow!

Augusta is for MAINE.
What Annapolis is to MARYLAND.
And Boston is for MASSACHUSETTS...

And **Lansing** (are you still listening?)
Is to the state of MICHIGAN.
MINNESOTA has Saint Paul.
But don't worry **Jefferson City**
Is the capital of beautiful MISSOURI!

MONTANA has beautiful **Helena** as its capital.
And Lincoln is the capital of NEBRASKA.
While **Carson City** brings NEVADA fame
And as for the capital of NEW HAMPSHIRE
Concord is the name!

NEW JERSEY claims **Trenton** as its capital.
And **Santa Fe** is the capital of NEW MEXICO.
While the capital of NEW YORK is **Albany**
And a beautiful place to go!

I know that NORTH CAROLINA has **Raleigh** as its capital.
And I remember **Bismarck** capitals NORTH DAKOTA.
(Did you remember too?)
And I know that OHIO has **Columbus** for its capital
(The one who sailed the ocean blue!)

Oklahoma City seems a natural
For the state of OKLAHOMA-yes, its the same.
While OREGON, with its Oregon Trails have fame,
Has a capital with **Salem** as its name

Betsy Ross made our first flag here
In PENNSYLVANIA with its rugged plateau.
And its capital is **Harrisburg**-
In case you didn't know!

RHODE ISLAND is so tiny,
But has a capital of Providence.
While SOUTH CAROLINA is next in line.
I like its capital of Columbia just fine!

The Rushmore state of SOUTH DAKOTA
Have you ever been there?
If so, you probably know
That its capital is Pierre.

Ya'll come to Nashville
The capital of TENNESSEE.
And you will soon find out
About southern hospitality.

TEXAS is a great big state
And I hear, Austin, its capital is great!
But of course in TEXAS.
Nothing is second rate!

UTAH with its snow-capped mountains
Is so clean and quiet and pretty.
And if you arrive in its capital
You will be in Salt Lake City!

As we are getting near the end.
I'm getting rather tired.
And to rhyme VERMONT'S Montpelier.
I'm finding rather hard!

I love the look of VIRGINIA.
It has some wonderful stories to share.
Some about the capital Richmond,
Which has grace and beauty to spare!

Olympia is the capital of WASHINGTON.
Which is way out on the coast.
Of all the luscious north western states-
Don't know which I love the most!

WEST VIRGINIA we're back to you
With Charleston as your best.
Thinking of the green countryside
And grassy mountains with which you're blessed!

We've really gone through so many states
And we must not leave out a single one.
So let's take a moment to appreciate.
Madison, the capital of WISCONSIN!

To end this little verse I've left
Cheyenne, WYOMING to the last.
But it is not the least of the states.
For it has a lot of class.

There, I hope I've said them all.
And not left one out of my rhyme.
But if I did just let me know.
I'll add it in-there's time!!

Everyone should know the states
Because this is where we live!
And if you learn them all-
A great big "A" I'll give!

The capitals are important
And so is their history...
Of when each state became a state.
And how the capital came to be!

What are:

Continents, Oceans, Seas, Rivers, and Topography?

Name the seven continents (in order of size:)

1. Asia
2. Africa
3. North America
4. South America
5. Antarctica
6. Europe
7. Australia/Oceania

Name the Countries

1. Africa – (53)
2. Europe – (46)
3. Asia – (44)
4. North America – (23)
5. Oceania – (14)
6. South America – (12)
7. Antarctica – (0)

*Note: In some parts of the world, students are taught that there are only six continents, as they combine North America and South America into one continent called Americas. Other experts use only six continents by combining Europe and Asia into a continent called Eurasia. Also, the numbers of countries may change over the years.

Asia is the largest continent and includes 44 countries and islands. In Asia, you will find the world's tallest mountain, Mt. Everest in Nepal and the most highly populated countries of China and India.

Africa is the planet's 2nd largest continent and includes 53 individual countries. It contains the Nile River, the world's longest, and the massive world's largest desert, the Sahara.

North America is the 3rd largest continent and includes Canada, Greenland, Mexico, the United States, the countries of Central America and the island countries and dependencies of the Caribbean. The continent's highest point is Mt. McKinley, in Alaska; the lowest point is Death Valley in California.

Antarctica is almost completely covered with ice. Antarctica is the coldest and windiest spot on the planet. The lowest temperature ever recorded on Earth was recorded in Antarctica.

Europe is the planet's 6th largest continent and includes 46 countries, and a few dependencies, territories and regions. Europe is really not a continent, but part of the peninsula of Euroasia, which includes all of Europe and Asia.

South America is the fourth largest continent and includes (12) countries and (3) major territories. The continent contains the Amazon River and rainforest, the Andes Mountains and some of the most spectacular scenery on the planet. Argentina, Bolivia, Brazil, Chili, Columbia, Ecuador, Guyana, Paraguay, Peru, Suriname, Uruguay, and Venezuela are the 12 countries. The three territories are Falkland Islands, French Guiana, and Galapagos Islands.

Australia/Oceania, is the smallest continent and combines all of Australia, New Zealand, Papua New Guinea, as well as the thousands of coral atolls and volcanic islands of the South Pacific Ocean, including the Melanesia and Polynesia groups as well as Micronesia, a widely scattered group of islands that run along the northern and southern edges of the Equator.

Oceans of the World:

1. Pacific
2. Atlantic
3. Indian
4. Southern
5. Arctic

About Oceans

Today we studied about oceans
And the way they affect our lives.
And yes, they affect everyone
Kids, moms, husbands and wives!

Great ships sail on the ocean
And kids play in the sand along the shore.
But there are great mysteries beneath its waves,
Would you like to learn some more?

Then listen carefully today
As we take a little trip,
As our books take us to the ocean-
Perhaps we'll take a dip!

Help With History

United States Presidents

Do you know the Presidents?
Can you name them everyone?
Let's take time to learn them.
I think you will find it fun!

How many Presidents have there been
Since the founding of our nation?
How many of their birthdays
Do we still honor with a celebration?

Do you know what states they came from?
Do you know how many served two terms and when?
So far there have been no women Presidents.
There have only thus far been men.

Can you name their wives?
Do you know which ones had kids?
Do you remember from modern newscasts
Specific things they did?

Let's take some time to study
And learn the facts about each one.
And you will find yourself caught up in history.
Before your quest for this knowledge is done!

🔑 Before you introduce the study of the Presidents, post paintings and photos around the room without identifying them and see how many the students will recognize. If you hint that there might be a small reward for the person who identifies the most, the students may start researching on their own to find the name that goes with the photo.

Board Smartz

1. George Washington. 1789-1797 "Father of His Country"

2. John Adams. 1797-1801 "Atlas of Independence"

3. Thomas Jefferson. 1801-1809 "Sage of Monticello"

4. James Madison. 1809-1817 "Father of the Constitution"

5. James Monroe. 1817-1825 "Era-of-Good-Feeling President"

6. John Quincy Adams. 1825-1829 "Old Man Eloquent"

7. Andrew Jackson. 1829-1837 "Old Hickory"

8. Martin Van Buren. 1837-1841 "The Red Fox of Kinderhook"

9. William Henry Harrison. 1841 "Old Tippecanoe"

10. John Tyler. 1841-1845 "His Accidency"

11. James Knox Polk. 1845-1849 "Young Hickory"

12. Zachary Taylor. 1849-1850 "Old Rough and Ready"

13. Millard Fillmore. 1850-1853 "The American Louis Philippe"

14. Franklin Pierce. 1853-1857 "Young Hickory of the Granite Hills"

15. James Buchanan. 1857-1861 "Old Buck"

16. Abraham Lincoln. 1861-1865 "Honest Abe"

17. Andrew Johnson. 1865-1869 None

18. Ulysses Simpson Grant. 1869-1877 "Hero of Appomattox"

19. Rutherford Birchard Hayes. 1877-1881 "Dark-Horse President"

20. James Abram Garfield. 1881 None

21. Chester Alan Arthur. 1881-1885 "The Gentleman Boss"

22. Grover Cleveland. 1885-1889 "Veto Mayor"

23. Benjamin Harrison. 1889-1893 "Kid Gloves Harrison"

24. Grover Cleveland. 1893-1897 "Uncle Jumbo". "Veto Mayor"

25. William McKinley. 1897-1901 "Idol of Ohio"

26. Theodore Roosevelt. 1901-1909 "TR". "Trust-Buster". "Teddy"

27. William Howard Taft. 1909-1913 None

28. Woodrow Wilson. 1913-1921 "Schoolmaster in Politics"

29. Warren Gamaliel Harding. 1921-1923 None

30. Calvin Coolidge. 1923-1929 "Silent Cal"

31. Herbert Clark Hoover. 1929-1933 None

32. Franklin Delano Roosevelt. 1933-1945 "FDR"

33. Harry S Truman. 1945-1953 "Give 'Em Hell Harry"

34. Dwight David Eisenhower 1953-1961 "Ike"

35. John Fitzgerald Kennedy. 1961-1963 "JFK"

36. Lyndon Baines Johnson. 1963-1969 "LBJ"

37. Richard Milhous Nixon. 1969-1974 None

38. Gerald Rudolph Ford. 1974-1977 "Jerry"

39. James Earl Carter. Jr. 1977-1981 "Jimmy"

40. Ronald Wilson Reagan. 1981-1989 "The Gipper"

41. George Herbert Walker Bush. 1989-1993 "Poppy"

42. William Jefferson Clinton. 1993-2001 "Bill"

43. George Walker Bush. 2001-Present "W". "Little George"

🔑 To reinforce the study-games such as Jeopardy or other current quiz shows will be fun for the students.

🔑 A question or thought of the day on the chalk board each morning could include information learned in this study.

🔑 Example: He was a recent president and his nickname was "The Gipper."

Name the Presidents

If I had been a kid about 1795.
It would be easy to name the presidents
For there had been only one and he was still alive!
George Washington
Became our first President in 1789.

And then. **John Adams** became the second.
After the "father of our country" had served his time.

You surely know the name of the "Sage of Monticello"
For **Thomas Jefferson** became our third president-
A mighty brilliant fellow!

James Madison. "Father of the Constitution."
Was the fourth to be selected
To hold this important office when in 1809.
By the people he was elected.

James Monroe became the fifth in 1817.
And his time in office was the "Era-of-Good-Feeling."

"Old Man Eloquent"
Was the name **John Quincy Adams** was known by.
When he became the sixth to hold the office. in 1825.

In 1829. **Andrew Jackson**. known as "Old Hickory."
Became the seventh to go down in our presidential history!

In 1838, **Martin Van Buren**,
Known as "The Red Fox of Kinderhook,"
Became the eighth president-
According to my history book!

William Henry Harrison,
"Old Tippecanoe" as he was defined,
Made our historical records in 1841,
As president number nine.

In 1841, **John Tyler**, "His Accidency,"
(Number ten) became a part
Of our nation's history
As he assumed, after Harrison's death,
The office of the presidency!

I wonder if **James Knox Polk**, of Tennessee,
Ever thought before 1845
That our eleventh president
He would someday be!

The twelfth president was **Zachary Taylor**,
"Old Rough and Ready,"
But died after he served only a short time,
And 141 years later the cause
They were still trying to define-
Was it arsenic? They wondered if it was so,
But years later scientists say no.

Presidently Speaking!

Millard Fillmore.
President number thirteen.
Elected in 1850.
Was nicknamed by some
"The American Louis Philippe."

Franklin Pierce.
Our fourteenth president, in 1853,
Was nicknamed "Young Hickory."

Fifteen presidents I've listed so far
As I add "Old Buck-**James Buchanan**, 1857
Can you remember who they are?
If you can remember all fifteen, then you deserve a star!

"Honest Abe" they called him!
In 1861, **Abraham Lincoln**,
Who was called a rail splitter.
But everyone soon knew his name—
When our sixteenth president he became.
And with his biography, we became fascinated
With the history of how in Ford's Theatre
He was assassinated.

Andrew Johnson.
In 1865, became president
And was our seventeenth one.
But compared to other countries
Our nation was very young.

Name that President!

Eighteenth president for our country in 1869.
Is a name you might know—
Ulysses Simpson Grant.
"The Appomattox hero!"
Now if someone asks you
Who is buried in Grant's tomb,
You will know—
It is **Ulysses S. Grant**.
Our nation's hero.

Our nineteenth was
Rutherford Birchard Hayes, 1877,
Called the "Dark-Horse President."
Who won the presidency by only one electoral vote.
A president winning by that amount
Should show us how each vote can count!

James Abram Garfield, 1881
Became president number twenty,
But was only in office for two-hundred days
When he was shot by a stalker and later died.
Makes one wonder what this man
Would have accomplished
If his shooting he would have survived.

Chester Alan Arthur, 1881,
Nicknamed "The Gentleman Boss,"
Then became president number twenty-one.
Not because of an election,
But because of a man with a gun!

Twenty-two presidents now you've learned
And another star you've earned!
With **Grover Cleveland**, "Veto Mayor," in 1885.
We remember that he accepted the Statue of Liberty
On behalf of the United States.
A gift that would have significance great!
And if you like sweets, the fact the candy bar "Baby Ruth"
Was named after his daughter, you might find neat!

Benjamin Harrison, 1889, "Kid Gloves Harrison"
Became president number **twenty-three**.
And by a very small vote
He won this White House victory!

Grover Cleveland, again at twenty-four,
Was the only president to serve
Two non-consecutive terms,
But this was his last term—
There weren't any more.

William McKinley, in 1897,
Our twenty-fifth president became.
Having been the governor of Ohio,
To them he had fame.
And so the "Idol of Ohio,"
Became his nickname.

To Govern Our Land With Justice

Theodore Roosevelt, 1901.

"Teddy" went from being vice president
To being elected President.
I guess he had learned a lot
From the VP time he'd spent!
You may have seen him standing 60 feet tall—
Our twenty-sixth president is on Mount Rushmore
In case you don't recall!
And one more thought I'd like to share.
Perhaps you have a "Teddy" Bear?

William Howard Taft.

Our twenty-seventh leader in 1909,
Was rather a hesitant president.
But seems he did just fine.
Later, President Harding made him
Chief Justice of the United States.
That to Taft, the appointment was
His greatest honor he made evident
When he said that made him
Forget that he was ever president!

Twenty-eight presidents.
If I add on **Woodrow Wilson**.
President from 1913 to 1921!
He wanted to keep the country safe
And was concerned for our welfare.
But soon he had to admit the need
To enter the war was there.

Warren Gamaliel Harding, 1921, our twenty-ninth,
Had some funny habits that you might want to look up–
You might not find them all in the history books!
He spoke his own idea of English,
Still called by some HARDING-SPEAK,
Because his use of words was quite unique!

Calvin Coolidge, "Silent Cal,"
In 1923 was elected,
Our thirtieth president to be
And a much beloved president was he.

Herbert Clark Hoover, our 31st was elected in 1929,
Within eight months of his inauguration,
The stock market crashed,
Signifying the beginning of the Great Depression,
The most severe economic crisis
The United States had ever known–
Did not create a good impression!

Franklin Delano Roosevelt,
32nd president, elected in 1933,
Was just called "FDR" by the country,
He told the country what they wanted to hear
That was nothing they should fear, but fear.

Harry S. Truman became our 33rd president,
In 1945, when our 32nd president died,
From being vice president to "FDR,"
Overnight he was the one in the limelight.

Dwight David Eisenhower who was known as "IKE,"
Was the 34th president of the United States
And strived for peace with all his might.

John Fitzgerald Kennedy,
Known as "JFK,"
Became our 35th president in 1961,
And the era known as Camelot had begun.
His life was taken by an assassination,
And the country was shocked
At the cruelty with which our president was shot.

Lyndon Baines Johnson, "LBJ,"
36th president, became our leader on that fateful day,
In 1963, when "JFK" was suddenly taken away.

The 37th president was
Richard Milhous Nixon in 1969,
Faced with what seemed almost certain impeachment,
As his trustworthiness seemed to decline.
Nixon announced on August 8, 1974, that he would resign.

Gerald Rudolph Ford
Was the 38th President of the United States.
Two different times assassination attempts were thwarted
And the Secret Service protection skills,
Were with his lack of injury, rewarded.

He Shall Lead With Truth

James Earl Carter, Jr. 1977.

Our 39th president. nickname was "Jimmy."
He had once been a Naval officer and also governor
Before his time was duly spent
In office of the president.

Ronald Wilson Reagan.

Who became our 40th president in 1981.
Had been an actor before his political career was begun.
But once he got involved with it-
Politics seemed to be what made him tick!

George Herbert Walker Bush.

Elected in 1989 as our 41st president.
Was sometimes called "Poppy."
He called for a "kinder and gentler nation"
And thought that would be a cause for celebration!

William Jefferson Clinton.

Our 42nd president. was the second U.S. president
To be impeached by the House of Representatives.
But a still popular holder of the office he continued to be.

Our 43rd president was
George Walker Bush.

Who began his term in 2001.
Yes. he was George Herbert's son!
He declared us to be in a state of war
And our country is still fighting thus far.

For more interesting facts visit:
http://www.potus.com

Being President

Being president
Must be a lot of fun.
When the day is over
And his work is done.

A president has so many
Neat things to do and see.
And has great adventures
Unavailable to you or me.

Being president is a goal
That I think I shall strive for.
I think it may be possible to reach—
I'm right on track, so far!

Other Activities

🔑 Have students do research of the US presidents and come up with some questions of their own. Have them search for unusual or little known facts that other students will have to search for in books or on books.

🔑 Ask students how many presidents have there been in office during their lifetime and how many they actually remember. Have students research on president and his family and be able to report to the class.

🔑 Place photos of the presidents on the board and the name of each one in order to help the students remember.

🔑 Have the students each be responsible for learning about one president. Then, have the class present them in order of the presidents.

Amazed by Animals

What fun to study animals and learn about their habitats and families. There are so many wonderful photos of animals available from magazines and the web in addition to the photos that students may have taken on trips or safaris with their families. Place photos on the board and do a study of one each week or several depending at a time.

Assign students to work as a team. Do the following for the board:

1. Draw a picture of the animal.
2. Locate the area on the map where the animal is found.
3. Research and report some interesting facts to the class concerning the animal.

The Panda

I love to watch the Panda Bear
Playing at the zoo.
I could stare at them all day
To see what they would do.

The beauty of the Panda
Is almost beyond compare.
God created a masterpiece
In the Panda Bear!

PANDAMONIAM is... not the love of pandas!

The Giraffe

Nature has many wonderful sights.
Lovely to behold.
None are lovelier to my eyes
Than giraffes of brown and gold.

Tall and lean they stand
On legs much taller than my head.
They would lose their mystery
If they stood on stubby legs instead!

So enjoy your bears and chipmunks
And cuddle those koala bears.
But when I go to the zoo or park,
The giraffe my deep affection shares!

I love the Hippopotamus

You never see a hippo make a fuss
Over things that bother us!
You never see one fuss and fume
If kids don't bathe or clean their room!

You never see one that's fussing at
An elephant, puppy dog or rat
Or telling his sibling she's a brat!
That's why I like the hippopotamus!

They're much to big to climb a tree
Or play tag or hide and seek with me.
But my happiness would never end,
If I had a hippo as a friend!

The Kangaroo

The kangaroo is a funny sight
With her legs on loose
And her ears on tight...
With great big feet
On the bottom
And tiny legs on top...
It's a wonder that a roo can hop!
A kangaroo is strange to see
With a pouch in front
To hold her baby...
Although a roo looks funny to some.
I guess she is beautiful to another one.
And when she looks at me or you,
She probably prefers the look of a kangaroo!

The Spider

A spider is a delicate masterpiece
That can spin a dainty web so wide
That can be so beautiful, yet strong
To catch its prey inside.

A spider is so misunderstood
By mankind here on earth.
It's just doing the task
For which it was designed at birth.

We watch in awe and wonder
As its magic web the spider weaves,
In hopes that some tasty insect
Its apparent fragility it would deceive.

Animals Self-Defense

People have various ways of defending themselves depending upon the situation. Bulletin boards can display animals, human and non-human. It's fun to describe their ways of self-defense.

🔑 Porcupines, lions, tigers, sharks, blowfish, shellfish, turtles, giraffes, skunks, deer, moose, crocodile, alligators, octopus, possums, rabbits, woodpeckers, electric eels, snakes, clams, gophers and birds

🔑 The display can be a large one with numerous animals or one animal at a time can be displayed and studied in depth.

Pity the Poor Porcupine

Oh, pity the poor porcupine-
He can't be a friend of mine.
For he has no place that I could pet
And what if he should
Per chance forget
And slap his tail-quills would fly!
Sticking in me as they went by!
I feel that I should be his friend.
If I knew I could depend
That he would keep his quills intact
And never his new friend attack.
But I think I'm much safer
After considering that.
By having as a pet, a dog or a cat!

Protection Comes In Many Forms

Animals must have a way of defense
To prevent themselves from being past tense!
A porcupine does just fine
By throwing out those prickly spines!
A tiger one does not suggest
Would welcome an unexpected guest.
For he is powerful, big and strong
And a smaller animal would not last long!
Sharks scare man and fish
Even though I hear
They make a tasty dish!
Playing possum works for this little critter
And some plants and animals
Have a taste that is bitter.
Clams and oysters have a hard shell
As does the turtle as well.
Gophers live in holes
As do some snakes and moles.
But snakes hiss and bite
And lions growl
There are horns so big
On the gentlest cow!
As I look around the world I see.
That so many animals are bigger than me.
But I have protection in many forms,
And don't depend on my skin to keep me warm.
I wear clothes depending on the season
And to defend myself I use my reason.

Whiff!

There once was a little furry creature
Sitting on a log looking so alone.
When I had just been wishing
For a pet to call my own!
It had a fluffy tail
With fur so smooth and black.
And seemed like a lovely pet to have
And I loved the white stripe down its little back!
But 'ere I chanced to pet it.
And turned away from me.
Soon the reason it was alone
Became apparent to see!
It lifted up its little tail
And before a word I could say.
The most awful stinky odor
Was swiftly sent my way!
This was my first experience
With the dainty little creature
That is known for
That one annoying feature!

What About the Opossum?

I heard a noise in the yard–
A rattling of our fence.
At first I couldn't see the culprit.
For he had a great defense.
He looked as if he were dead–
His expertise at staying still
Was absolutely awesome!
But merely "playing possum!"

Artistically Speaking

Here is My Work

Here is a painting that I did!
I hope you like the way it looks
For it is unique and original—
Not found in any book!

Sharing Your Work

Please feel free to paint and draw
Your idea of what you saw.
I won't insist
That you color within the lines
Or second guess your great designs.

We will post them on the board
Especially to share with each other.
And when Parent's Day comes around,
We will show them to your Dad and Mother.

Today we drew animals
To share with one and all.
We also drew signs of the seasons
Winter, Summer, Spring and Fall.

Below we display our artwork
And hope it will make you smile,
Help you to relax and enjoy
Using your imagination for a while.

Display the children's artwork and some little verses.

Extracurricular Activities

Be a Good Sport!

My parents don't care
If I am not the best at basketball
Or don't make the football team.
But rather they want me to excel
As a very nice human being.
My friends don't mind if I cheer from the sidelines
As they go through their paces,
Making touchdowns, scoring goals
Making baskets or winning races.
And I don't need to excel
At every sport I do.
But I need to know that in every thing,
My good sportsmanship shines through.

Sports to Ponder

What sports do you enjoy?
What can you find out about the greats in that sport?
How did that sport get started?
Is this sport as popular in other countries?

🔑 Have kids bring photos of themselves participating in sports either at school or in the summer. Post the photos and create a hall of fame for them no matter what the activity or degree of participation. Non-athletic kids can be designated as fans and cheer squad. Do this as icebreakers and teamwork exercise.

Being a Team Player!

What Did You Do This Summer?

What did you do this summer?
What did you do for fun?
Did you play softball with the gang?
Or touch football in the sun?

Were you always at the swimming pool
Or did you go to a lake?
Did you play soccer or badminton
Or some classes did you take?

Bring a photo to share with the class
And we will post them on the wall.
So that we can enjoy not just one sport.
But can learn more about them all!

The Athlete

An athlete is a special person
With strength of body and soul.
It takes a lot of inner strength
To retain his outer control.

His mind is sharp and his body strong.
His focus never wavers
As he starts for his final goal.
And every moment he savors.

Whether in a practice session
Or in a scheduled meet.
Or running countless marathons.
He's ready to compete.

Through the Months...

January

Snow in the eastern states. New Year's. Winter.
Martin Luther King, Jr.'s Birthday

February

Ground Hog Day. Black History Month. Valentine's Day.
President's Day. Leap Year

March

St. Patrick's Day. Beginning of Spring

April

Easter Holidays. Earth Day. Spring arrives

May

Mother's Day. Graduations. Memorial Day

June

Flag Day. Father's Day. Summer arrives

July

Independence Day. Picnics. Summer. Sunshine

August

Back-to-School. Last picnics and campouts

September

Labor Day. Grandparent's Day. Fall arrives

October

Fall. Halloween. Harvest

November

Elections. Thanksgiving. Veteran's Day

December

Christmas. Hanukah. Kwanzaa. Winter arrives

It's January!

It's January and wouldn't you know
The weather is cold and we have SNOW!

We celebrate this **Happy New Year**
As midnight approaches on December 31st
And people dawn their party hats and whistles
Long before it hits 11:30!

Our calendar has a day marked in red.
The birthday of a man who led.
He wasn't a president but he was a strong man
Who marched with his people hand in hand.
He spent his life trying to make freedom ring
And we will remember always **Martin Luther King.**

Yes. it is winter here in the United States
But if in the western states you make your home.
You don't have the fun of building snowmen
Unless to the high mountains you choose to roam.

It's January!

We have a brand new calendar
With pages fresh and new.
A fresh slate to write on
And to show what we can do!
Amid the shouts of celebration
Wishing us a **Happy New Year-**
Could those be the sounds
Of resolutions I hear?

February is Fabulous

Hip Hip Hooray!
February second is Ground Hog Day!
If the little critter comes out
And sees his shadow in the sun,
Then winter isn't over yet...
There are 40 more days to come!

I love the fact that Valentine's Day
Is just around the bend,
For I have a lot of people
To whom cards I'd love to send!

I always remember my teacher
And my best friends in my grade,
And especially love to send my mom
A valentine that I've made!

Presidents Lincoln and Washington
Were born in this shortest month of the year.
Both of them shared many words of wisdom
To those who were smart enough to hear.

We celebrate Black History Month
And embrace our diversity,
And all of the ethnicities
That help our country to be all it can be!

Leapin' into a New Year

Marvelous March

How could we not mention,
And celebrate in style,
The birthday of Dr. Seuss,
A man who made us smile!

To celebrate St. Patrick's Day!
I will draw a shamrock
And wear a hat of green,
And be the cutest leprechaun
The world has ever seen!

April Showers

The birds are singing and the
Flowers are blooming
And there is just so much to see...
It is only natural that on Arbor Day,
I should want to plant a tree!!

April showers bring May flowers
That's what the poets say,
That's why I think that Summer
Should have one more holiday!!

May Brings the Flowers

Let's remember that Mother's Day
Always comes around in May
And honor our Mothers or someone dear
On this special day of the year!

June is Jumping

Father's Day comes in June
And we must go to the store
To find something unique and grand.
And befitting my Dad. a wonderful man!

On June 15th. Flay Day comes along—
We should be ready to sing
A rousing patriotic song!

July is Independence Day

I love the parades and excitement
Of Independence Day each year!
It is a happy celebration
Of the Freedoms we hold dear!

August is Awesome

August is here and I am so loving Fall.
But alas. I hear the Back-to-School call!
But the Olympics are always going on.
And they encourage me to grow up to be strong.

September

Hip Hip Hooray you all.
It is the return of Fall!
Look at the leaves!
Look at the colors so cool—
September really is a jewel!

October is a Fright!

BOO! I can be the scariest sight you've seen
When October brings Halloween!
Fall and Harvest time are here
And we think of folks
Both far and near.

November is Neat!

Thanksgiving time is here at last-
The school year is going fast.
And depending on the year,
Sometimes it means
That presidential elections are here!
Soon we will elect a new White House resident
To serve as our new president

December is Delicious!

I think we all remember
Our favorite holiday in December!

What other Holidays can you list?

_____
_____
_____
_____
_____
_____
_____

🔑 Have a calendar on the wall or bulletin board each month for not only well known holidays, but let kids research and suggest other lesser known ones. Let them be responsible for suggesting ways to celebrate or decorate for them. Also, put each child's birthday on the calendar so that everyone can share in the holiday excitement!

Learning From Simple Things

Teachers don't always have the latest and greatest in supplies or equipment. While some schools may have abundance and computers in each classroom, others may have only meager supplies. I have always believed that you can find a lesson in anything. Look around you at the simple things and create a bulletin board using that to teach about various subjects. You might ask a student to donate something for the board and then, see what you can find out about it. Objects such as ribbon, hair clips, leather belts, cookies, pencils, etc. all have a history of sorts. Things like value, place of origin, cost to manufacture, artistic value or food value.

We can learn from simple things
That we use every day
Look around you as you study
And view things in a different way!

🔑 Bring a plate or box of cookies to share with the class. Put a large picture of a cookie on the board or draw it on the blackboard.

What Can We Learn From A Cookie?

Art: A cookie is aesthetically pleasing, has a nice circular shape that can be decorated in various ways and can even be decorated with photos and words.

Math: Define the shape of a cookie. What is a circle and how do you measure a circle? What is circumference? What is width? How can the cookie be equally divided for 5 people?

Health: What is the nutritional value of the cookie? What ingredients went into it and how can you make it into a more nutritionally sound cookie?

Entertainment: Who is the Cookie Monster?

Geography: Where do ingredients such as chocolate, peanuts, vanilla flavoring, sugar, etc. come from. What countries or states supply us with the ingredients for the cookies?

🔑 Bring a plate or box of cookies to share with the class. Put a large picture of a cookie on the board or draw it on the blackboard.

What Can We Learn From A Spinning Top?

Try your hand and see what subjects and lessons "turn up."
What modern conveniences work on the same principle?
Why does it suddenly stop and crash?
What about tops in history?
What makes a top spin?
How fast can a top go?
What is a gyroscope?
What is a Dreidle?

**I'm a little top
What makes me spin?
What makes me stop
Or start again?**

What Can You Learn From A Dollar Bill?

I'm just a little piece of cotton and linen blend
With a president on my front.
Do you know what is on my back?
I am a dollar bill, but for "cents" I do not lack.

Art: Look at the unique design of the dollar bill. Have kids design a dollar bill of their own.

History: Whose photo is on the bill? When was he elected president and what was his nickname? Where was he from?

Math: How many pennies, nickels, dimes, quarters, or half dollars make up the one dollar bill? What number do you see represented over and over in the design? (Hint: Some people think it is an unlucky number.)

Language skills: What mottos do you find on the bill? What other languages do you see represented? What are those phrases?

Now that you know a bit
About that little piece of paper
That you take to the store.
Does it make you like it more?

Does knowing a bit about its history
Make you feel like it's a mystery?
Does it cause you to want to learn
More about the cash you earn?

What Can You Learn From a Skunk?

I'm a really cute little stinker
(*Mephitis, mephitis*)
And I try very hard to be polite.
Although when I approach,
Folks run away in fright.

Art: Draw a skunk

Biology: What is the scientific name? Description? What do they eat? How do they bear their young? How does it protect itself? What is its main predator?

Geography: Where do skunks live? What can you learn from the world map?

Math: How many babies does a mommy skunk give birth to at once? How far can the skunk spray it's odor? What is it's size? How many toes do they have?

Little Stinker

The skunk is so adorable
In his suit of black and white.
And rather difficult to see
In the darkness of the night.
But it has a special talent
Which serves it very well.
A very unique protection—
A really awful smell!

What Can We Learn From Colors?

What About Colors

If I'm feeling sad and dreary
And need to express that to you
I don't say I'm feeling green.
But that I'm feeling blue!

When we see a red light.
We know that we should stop.
Because if we go on through it
We will have to face a cop!

But green allows us to go ahead.
And yellow tells us that caution we should use.
We must obey each of them
Or our licenses we will lose.

Purple denotes royalty and power
And white is worn by American brides.
And in our American Flag–
Red. White and Blue are side by side.

Black people aren't really black.
Neither are white folks white.
But we are mostly overlapping shades of brown
If you want to get it right!

Some colors carry symbolism
That started very long ago.
Stirring up our feelings of pride or patriotism
And when we see them. their meanings we know.

continued...

Some colors are comforting like counting sheep
And may soothe us and lull us into sleep.
Some colors may make us feel sad,
While others make us happy and glad!

I love the whole rainbow of colors
I love their awesome sight.
And I just cannot imagine
A world of only black and white.

World Without Color

I cannot imagine a world
Without color.
A world where the grass
Was not green.
A world where the colors in the sky
Were not the beautiful colors
I've seen.

I cannot imagine a world without color.
Where the blues of the sky above
Were not reflected in the
Beautiful eyes
Of the ones that
I so dearly love!

Thank God for the beautiful colors.
For the green grass and the sky so blue.
Thank God for the beautiful colors.
Thank God for the wonder of you!

🔑 What can you learn from colors?

🔑 Color is the by-product of the spectrum of light.

What Can You Learn From Soda Pop?

What makes it so noisy?
What is the fizz and hissing sound?

Soda Should Only Pop

I opened up my can of pop
And I heard an awful sound.
I thought a cat was in the room
And so I looked around!

It hissed and fizzed and acted strange
And scared me out of my skin.
Until it finally stopped,
And all was quiet again!

I like my soda to be quiet
And not make a bit of noise.
I don't think a hissing sound
Is something anyone enjoys!

So next time when I want a soda pop,
Mom, I will depend on you—
To open it up and pour it in a cup
Until all it's hissing is through!

🔑 The hiss is the sound of carbon dioxide gas escaping from the bottle. This gas is under pressure and it is this pressure that keeps the soda carbonated. Carbonation is what gives the soda pop its fizz.

There is a lot of science in our sodas!

If you shake a soda, the gas which was at the top is mixed through the soda, and when you stop, most of this gas returns to the top of the container. Small bubbles of the gas get stuck all over the sides of the bottle, and when the bottle is opened, these bubbles expand very quickly and try to force their way up and out of the bottle. They push through the soda to the top and force soda out of the bottle in a very explosive manner!

To prevent this from happening you can tap the sides of the container which knocks the trapped bubbles off the sides of the bottle allowing them to collect at the top of the bottle. Then, you can open the can without a spray of soda.

Pop Pop Fizz Fizz

If you drop a soda,
Don't pick it up in a hurry,
Or about a slight eruption–
You will have to worry!

The bubbles will expand
And rush up to the top,
Then you will be unable
Their escape to stop!

So tap the sides lightly,
And this is the easy way–
To open the bottle safely
And avoid a soda spray!

Oh, how delicious The taste of it is!

What Can You Learn From a Butterfly?

Art: The butterfly is so lovely to look at and easy to draw. Students from the earliest years feel comfortable drawing the simple shape and filling with color. Students can draw butterflies and post them for an art project. Some may want to use their computer skills and scan them to print on other items such as calendars or wearable art.

Science/Biology: Butterflies are beautiful, flying insects with large scaly wings. The bulletin board can be a place to place a large butterfly and trace each of its stages with descriptions and definitions.

The Butterfly

Who would think that an egg laid on a leaf
Would turn into an insect beautiful beyond belief!
The larva (caterpillar) hatches from the egg
And eats leaves and flowers as it molts and grows—
Doing this many times the biologist knows.

Molting is what we call losing its old skin
As it becomes too small.
We may spot a larva in this stage,
But may not have seen them all.

The larva turns into a pupa (chrysalis)
And takes a little rest
Until the resting stage is done,
And then, the resulting beautiful adult emerges
As a butterfly and a very beautiful one!

Geography: Where do you find butterflies?

Butterflies are found all over the world
To be enjoyed by every boy and girl!
In all types of environments, you will find them there
In hot and cold, and dry and moist air.
At sea level and high in the mountains,
The butterflies can be found.
The world is much more beautiful
With butterflies around!

History: Fossils of butterflies are rare, but some have been found in the Cretaceous period back when dinosaurs roamed the earth.

What is A Butterfly?

A butterfly is easy to spot,
But made from butter-it is not!
It is an insect that is so true,
But it is so beautiful
For all of us to view!
With beautiful wings
Covered with colorful scales,
From plant to plant
In my garden they sail.
Pollinating plants as they go,
They are very important
To our world, you know!
Our world would not be
Nearly as lovely
Without butterflies
Flitting above me!

Looking into Language

Looking into Grammar

Where is Your **Grammar**?
(No, she isn't upstairs taking a nap!)
What are the **Parts of Speech**?
Today we learn the parts of speech.
I see no need to wait.
If you listen carefully,
You will see that there are **eight**!
Eight parts of speech such as the **noun**
That names a person place or thing,
And **verbs** which are action words
Like sing or dance or ring.
Adjectives are words that modify a noun
Or **pronouns** (another part of speech)
While **adverbs** modify verbs.
And then, there is the **preposition**,
Of which I'm sure you've heard.
It links the words together
By showing a relationship,
Such as the book is UNDER the table
Or the sailor is ON the ship.
Conjunctions have a function
So useful is the work they've done.
They link our words together
And make writing much more fun.
OH! I forgot the **interjection**!
Which is used to express emotion,
I use them frequently,
So they have my devotion.

93

To Be Grammatically Correct...

Remember that a **noun** is a person, place or thing.

A **pronoun** can take its place while an **adjective** tells about them, either one, and **verb** lets them have some action fun.

Adverbs are used to (modify) tell how they acted with prepositions showing the relationship of the noun (or pronoun or phrases) to the rest of the sentence.

The **conjunction** connects two things and the interjection allows you to exclaim!!

- 🗝 Use the board or chalkboard to have students list examples of each part of speech.

- 🗝 What is a sentence?

Every complete sentence contains two parts: a subject and a predicate. The **subject** is what (or whom) the sentence is about, while the **predicate** tells something about the subject.

The **simple predicate** is the verb of the sentence.

A **sentence** will always have a subject and a verb, but although that sounds really good sometimes the subject is (You) understood (Run! Walk! Stop!)

Ahhhh!
The Thrill of Language!
Add them together
to form a little story.

The ABC's of a Paragraph

With letters from the alphabet.
You form words and then.
Put those words together
As a complete thought
With a period at the end.
With those sentences you've formed.
Add them together to form a little story.
And there you have a PARAGRAPH
In all its glory!

Making Our Words Longer and Shorter

We make our words longer by adding prefixes and suffixes to the root word and we shorten them by taking letters away and adding an apostrophe to show that a letter is missing.

Prefixes: pre- un- dis- re- mis- im- bi- de- en–

Suffixes: -er -able -ous -ful -ly -or -y –ment –ing

joyful...enjoy...joyous

Create New Words With the Words Below:

work. friend. day. school. age. tear. love. full

What are Prefixes?   What are Suffixes?

We can add prefixes to the beginning
of a root word. and suffixes to the end.

write...rewrite...writer

What Are Roots?

On this board you see tree roots,
Without which trees could not exist.
Notice how they burrow into the earth
And how they turn and twist.

We as people have roots–
Our ancestors from way back.
Some attribute all of our good traits to them,
And some blame them for what we lack.

Our teeth have roots
Inside our gums,
And there are roots
For each baby tooth that comes.

The roots bring nourishment
To the teeth above
And keep well nourished
That beautiful smile we love!

All plants have roots
In one form or another
And some are the food we eat
Encouraged to do so by our mother.

Nails have roots and some roots
Are "square"
And if you pull one out
You will find a root on hair!

See what kind of roots you can find
And other things the word might mean
And you will find that even words have roots
That's how they came into being!

🔑 Picture displayed should be a tree with a large root support system underground or a diagram of the inside of a tooth.

🔑 Have the children bring in family photos for a family tree project.

What Are Root Words?

Root words are words that stand alone
With nothing added to beginning or end
You can create many by adding
To a word like friend.

Friendless, friendly, friendlier
All have that one trait.
They began with a single *friend*
And new words we chose to make.

Some words have their roots
In Latin or in Greek.
We may be using words created
From languages we don't speak!

Now look very closely
At the words you use today,
And figure out the beginning roots
Of the things you choose to say!

Get into your Roots!

Contractions

Words are really funny
And there are things we can do
To make them longer or shorter
And let their meaning still shine through.
We add prefixes to the beginning
And suffixes to the end.
And we can take part of the word out
And put an apostrophe in.

A "d" added to the word "I"
Can mean "I would" or "I had"
Or even "I would. I'd. I've. I'll.
Tell what I am doing."
"He'd" or "they'll" or "we'll" tell about others.
We can also use contractions with verbs
To create a different word.

Aren't means are not.
Would've is would have.
Could've is could have.
Hasn't is has not.
While weren't is were not.
And while do not is don't.
Will not becomes won't!
And that is not all...there are a lot!
Can you list some more?

🔑 List a group of words on the board and have the
students tell what two words make up the contraction.

We can use contractions for words such as:
not. would. had. should. will. have. is

What are Homonyms?

Sometimes words look exactly like another.
But have entirely different meanings from each other
And we call them **Homonyms**.

So we must remember this
When we read or write
Or else our stories would be a sight!

*bass, bowl, close, cobbler, does, file, flounder,
grave, hawk, list, minute, object, paddle , present, sow*

So a *bass* singer can fish for *bass*
And paddle there in his boat
If it doesn't start to *list*
But if it does he might insist
As he paddles to shore
That it be added to his *list*!

What are Homophones?

While others may sound alike
but have a different spelling and meaning—
these are called **Homophones**.

*board, bored, coarse, course, council, counsel, creak, creek,
knot, not, lead, led, ring, wring, who's, whose.*

For Instance...

A bored knight can ride out at night
And walk his horse across a board.
While the horse's feet may cause a creak,
As across the creek he urges the steed forward.

continued...

His fair lady who wears his ring may wring her hands
As she watches for her knight and sees him not.
But whose heart is happy when he appears,
Because her stomach has been tied in knots!

So if homonyms and homophones
You should start to confuse.
Just remember that the spelling and meaning
Are the clues to decide which is which for you.

A homonym will look the same
Like a bass who swims in the lake.
And the bass singer who entertains us
And whose song keeps us awake!

While a homophone may seem bizarre as the
bazaar in which you shop.
But once you are led to follow my lead,
It will be hard to stop.

Homonyms and Homophone-
They just won't leave my brain alone!
I see them in a book I've read
And sometimes dream of them in bed!

I sometimes think I have them straight
And their differences appreciate.
But then I think of other words,
Like here and hear and herd and heard...

And straight away my mind is zooming
With all kinds of interest looming.
As I try my very best
To figure them out before my test...

What Are Antonyms and Synonyms?

Synonym means "the same"

Antonym means "the opposite"

What are Heteronyms?

Heteronyms are words that are spelled the same but have different meanings when pronounced differently.

For example:

Lead, pronounced LEED, means to guide.
However, lead, pronounced LED, is a metal.

Review

Homographs are words that are spelled the same but differ in meaning, derivation, or pronunciation.

Homophones are words that are pronounced the same but differ in meaning, derivation, or spelling.

Homonyms are words that are spelled and pronounced the same but have different meanings. There is overlap among these categories.

Heteronyms are homographs in which the different pronunciations have different meanings. Many heteronyms are the result of one pronunciation being a verb and another being a noun.

🔑 See how many of each of the above you can list. Bring in a newspaper and rewrite a story using all of the above.

What We Want to Know

This is a good place for all of those questions that kids ask right when we are in the middle of something else. You can put these questions on the wall or a special board or have students write down questions and put them in a jar or box on your desk. Each day you can pull out a question to answer. The students can, then, help you research the more difficult or technical questions. The answers can be simple and age appropriate. Be prepared for strange and wonderful questions! You may get "Where do babies come from?" or "Why is the grass green?" But it will give you more insight as to what they are thinking and how their minds work. You can reserve the right to disregard any inappropriate questions.

Where We Find Answers

🔑 Teach the students how to use various research tools in an effective way. The internet is such a wonderful research tool to use often. However, also encourage the students to use the library and the vast amount of knowledge stored within its walls.

🔑 Students need to learn to use only facts as they research and not be taken in by works based on a real person or historical event.

🔑 Students should be encouraged to read and enjoy works of fiction and fantasy, but be able, even from a young age, to tell the difference.

Fiction, Fantasy, Fact or Lie?

There are things that are untrue
And you know their term so well.
You may call them untruths or lies,
And lies you should not tell.

Then there are whole books written
That are not totally fact.
There are some parts of truth in them
But they fill in what they lack.

They calls these books works of fiction
And they do not claim to be true.
But the writers love to pen them
Just to provide reading fun for you.

Then there are works so off the wall
Where no real truth lies within them.
But are created just at the authors whim—
To set your wildest imagination free
Which you may know as fantasy!

Always tell the truth each day
And unless a publisher comes your way
Asking that you write a piece to entertain
From the other three, please, refrain.

Remember

Encyclopedias and the media are fun things to know about
And the internet is helpful, that's without a doubt.
Listening to those around us, you will most assuredly find,
Improves the art of hearing and educates our mind!

Fact or Fiction Board

🔑 On the bulletin board, put book covers from Fiction, Historical Works, Fantasy and perhaps copies of well known gossip magazines or tabloids and have the students discuss the differences in each one.

🔑 Place copies of current news magazines for older students and discuss the way modern news is presented and the way it might be presented in, soon to be, history books.

🔑 For the lower grades, use students' favorite story books and talk about if the stories could actually happen. This board could also be tied in with good citizenship and manners.

What Would Happen If...?

🔑 This could be a fun board of fact, fun and fantasy as the students ask, "What would happen if...?" Suggest their own answers. Topics could be from science, math, language or history. Let them be creative and exercise their imaginations. Draw out the serious or the silly.

🔑 What would happen if cats had wings, dogs laid eggs and whales had four feet? What would happen if we dug a hole deep enough...would we really get to China? What would happen if there were no more chocolate or peanuts? What if farmers all grew the same crop one year? What would happen if ducks could no longer swim or dogs purred like cats or fish could stay out of water?

Opposites

🔑 What are opposites? We use them everyday.

🔑 Have students list as many opposites as they can think of.

🔑 Make a list of some of the harder ones to remember and place them on the board with the matching opposites having interlocking pieces that only fit the correct answer.

Opposite of What?

Some things mean the same thing
But are different words we say.
And other words mean entirely different.
Such as work and play!
We call these words opposites
And from morning until night.
We use words that are opposites
Such as left and right!
Some things are good
And some are bad.
Sometimes we are happy
And sometimes we are sad!
Home can be a castle
Or it can be a hut.
A pet can be pedigreed
Or it can be a mutt!
Food can be hot
Or some can be served cold.
And outfits that we wear
Can be new or old.

...continued

...continued from previous page
Some things are on top
And some are on the bottom.
Talk about opposite—
I'm sure you've got them!
Some dishes are clean
And some are dirty.
Some people are shy and demure
And others are flirty.
Some animals are tame
While some are wild.
And some people are adults
While another is a child.
Sometimes we get to work
And other times we play.
Some work at night
While others work all day.
Opposites are rather fun
And listing them is a breeze—
Just think about what you did today
And they will come with ease.

Do Opposites Really Attract?

Hyperbole Bulletin Board

Hyperbole is a figure of speech which is an exaggeration. His feet were as big as boats. Her dog was as big as an ox. We nearly died laughing. We sang until our lips fell off. He turned as white as a sheet. He was as tall as the maple tree! If I've told you once, I've told you a million times!

Such statements are not literally true. but people make them to sound impressive or to emphasize something. such as a feeling. effort. or reaction. Hyperboles are common in everyday language and in poetry and help create interesting stories.

This can help students in their creative writing by giving them examples of fun in their stories. Have each student suggest an example of some common hyperbole.

Is Your Glass Half-Empty or Half-Full?

Health-This bulletin board can be used to find the value of being a positive person.

Art-Draw examples of things that can be half-full and half-empty. Think outside the glass!

Language-How do you decide which is which? Is there a negative connotation in each time you use the word "empty"? Try telling someone a story using. first. one and then. the other.

🔑 Example: You are driving along on the freeway and your gas gauge says half a tank remains. How do you tell the story? "Oh. my goodness. our tank is half-empty!" "Oh. don't worry. our gas tank is still half-full!" Discuss the effect each sentence would have on your enjoyment or stress level.

🔑 "The kids drank some milk for a snack. but the glass was still half-full when they left." "The kids drank half a glass of milk with one cookie!"

🔑 Have the students write papers for the board with one paragraph concentrating on the positive and the other on the negative.

🔑 What other things can you think of that can be equally positive or negative in their appeal? Rain? "The rain will water all of the flowers and make the outdoors clear and fresh!" "Oh, no! It is going to rain again!" "It has rained every weekend!"

Positively Full

I'm a very positive person.
People all the time.
Like to be around me
And be a friend of mine!

I never see the negative
For positives are the best.
And to me the glass is half-full.
I don't hesitate to confess!

The rain is always welcome
To bring flowers in the spring.
And I love the little pigeons
As well as birds that sing!

My friends are always happy
When they see me enter the room.
For with my half-full take on life
There is no room for gloom!

Next time you see an empty glass,
Don't let it make you ill.
Just think of it as a pretty glass
That you have yet to fill!

Positives and Negatives

🔑 Can you show how to determine which is the positive and which is the negative end of a battery?

🔑 What are positives and negatives in photography? What are they in numbers?

🔑 Positive can also mean "sure" as in, "I am positive that I saw him!" And negative can mean "no" as in, "Negative, I didn't see him."

🔑 Life needs both positives and negatives, but as a person, we try to find positive things even in negative situations. This is illustrated in the old question of, "Is the glass half-full or half-empty?"

🔑 Without negatives, we wouldn't have things that run on batteries, no film photographs and so many other things. Also, the negative events in our daily lives can make us even more appreciative of the positive.

- 💡 Batteries have a positive and negative charge.
- 💡 Numbers have positive and negatives.
- 💡 People are described as positive and negative.
- 💡 Photography has positives and negatives.
- 💡 And of course there is YES and NO!

Are You Legible?
Our Handwriting is Important

The border of the bulletin board can be decorated in pens, pencils and old fashioned writing utensils. The inside, or heart of the board, should display the very best examples of the students handwriting.

🔑 Depending upon their age. you might want to get some practice sheets and examples of cursive writing to help students improve their writing skills.

🔑 I know there are companies that sell worksheets that you can use to trace over the letters to help you get a good start on cursive.

🔑 With the advent and popularity of computers for the entire family. handwriting seems to be lost in the shuffle and more and more people rely on fonts to speak for them. Our handwriting is something that is so uniquely us and should be practiced and improved. Who knows. our students may someday want to write a love note and they will want to make sure their intended can read it!

🔑 Have the students practice writing a poem on a lined piece of paper and then. try writing it on unlined and decorating the page for inclusion on the bulletin board.

🔑 For younger students. the exercise can be done with manuscript writing.

Flegible the Illegible

There was once a lad named Flegible
Whose writing was quite illegible.
He tried to write writing that could be read.
But the letters would not form in his head.
Fleggie was so frustrated and perplexed
That all of his letters looked like an "X."
Poor Flegible worked and stressed and groaned.
And under his weight his pencil moaned
As he pushed and shoved and gave it a twist
Until one day Flegible sprained his wrist!

...continued from previous page

Then, finally, his teacher when seeing his dismay,
Gave him some worksheets to help him one day.
Flegible made circles, ovals and spirals galore...
Soon they were perfect
And then he made some more!
Now Fleggie makes writing that can be read
And reads writing that others
Have written instead.
His teacher is now proud of his work each day
As Flegible sends writing he's written her way.

🔑 As your students improve their penmanship, you may find their desire or willingness to do more writing with pencil or pen and ink increases.

🔑 Have students create some beautiful handwritten letters to show off their new writing skills.

My Writing

I used to hate to write
And my writing was a sight!
If I had the need to read
The things I had written,
It all looked like hen scratches
Or the paw scratches of a kitten!
But once I practiced a bit
I found a pen that would fit,
And I moved it with such grace
That I soon found my place
And with my writing, now I am smitten!

Wow! Writing is Exciting !

Better a Letter

At the very first of the letter,
Is our **return address**
To show the person our town!
Then, we write the **date** to
Show when we wrote it down.
A **salutation** or **greeting** follows,
Which is another way to say, "hello."
And though it is usually "Dear Mr. or Mrs."
First names are fine for friends you know.
The **body** of the letter is the most important part
In which you can discuss your news
Or even works of art.
And when you want to sign off-
A **closing** is called for
Which can be, "Yours truly,"
And then, you tell them in the **signature**
Just who you are!

🔑 A good exercise is to have the students write thank you notes for their birthday or Christmas gifts.

🔑 They can also write to pen pals in other schools or in other countries.

🔑 Have students write a letter to their parents telling them about their class project and send it to their house. Oh, the excitement of mail in the mailbox!

🔑 Sometimes you will find a letter is better than most anything, because of all the wonderful thoughts and feelings it can bring.

Use All Your Senses to Write a Story

🔑 Write a dull story and post in on the board surrounded by strips of paper with words such as sight, smell, touch, hear, taste. Ask the students to rewrite the story using each of those senses.

🔑 Example: When I went to the park to play on the swings and slides I met some friends and we had cookies and milk for a nice snack.

🔑 Ask the students questions about the story they are going to rewrite in their own words. Encourage them to expand as much as they wish on the story. What and who did you see, what did you smell? Was the air fresh?

🔑 Describe the taste of your snack. What sounds did they hear at the park and what did the grass or sand feel like to their hands or feet?

🔑 A bulletin board that lists the five senses.

🔑 Let students use each sense when viewing items.

Your Senses

I have five senses
And I use them each day.
I used my eyes to see.
I use my ears to hear,
And my nose to smell.
And when I touch something-
What it is I can tell.
My other sense won't let chocolate go to waste-
My fifth sense is the one of taste!

Writing Workshop Board

(List on the board)

- ☀ What Does a Story Need?
- ☀ How Do I Get Started?
- ☀ What Characters Do I Need?
- ☀ What is Your Favorite Story?
- ☀ What Makes it Your Favorite?

🔑 On big bits of construction paper or cardstock, list some ideas for storylines, heroes, heroines, characters, locations, etc. Have the students arrange them into possible stories. Create enough options to make it fun for them to vary their choice of stories.

🔑 When working with these suggestions, you can adjust them to fit your grade level from primary to upper levels with minor changes. Board suggestion with kittens, could become boards with tigers and lions, boards with a cute honey bee, can become boards with a hive of realistic bees, and cute cartoon cars, can become hot wheels or race cars.

The Story
What does it need?
Where do I start?
Who is the hero?
Does he have heart?

Stepping Up Your Writing

🔑 Use cutouts, photos, drawings or books, such as a dictionary. For topic inspiration, use the Thesaurus and Encyclopedia to write the same story at a higher level. Use these books to find more powerful and grade appropriate words, or just to flesh out the simplest stories or verses.

(An example of stepping it up)

Simple Story

I bought a dog.
I took him home
And gave him water
And a big old bone.
He howled all night
And he ran away.
But he came back home
After just one day.

Up A Step

Fluff was a tiny little dog-
The cutest little pup.
I knew he was our dog
The first time I picked him up.
He barked all day with happiness
And then he howled all night.
The door was left opened and he ran outside.
Giving us quite a fright!
We were so very happy
When Fluff did reappear.
That we gave him lots of hugs
And I kissed his little ear.

115

Up One More Step

A dog was the last thing
We thought we would take home
When we got that call
On the telephone.
A friend had a mommy dog
With one puppy too many to keep.
She said she thought we might like one.
And we thought we would just take a peek-
But when we saw that puppy face.
Our hearts were full of joy.
This was our pup. our ball of fluff-
Our little puppy boy!
Not accustomed to puppies in the home.
The front door we left ajar.
And down the street our Fluffy went.
But he didn't go very far.
Even though he was new to the neighborhood.
Our Fluffy was very smart
It was as if he had learned immediately
Directions back to our hearts!

🔑 On the board put examples of writing that has been stepped up and have students discuss what the difference is in each sample.

Thesaurus— What's Another Word for it?

Our Day At The Park

Today we went to the park.
The green and flower-filled park.
Where the air smells fresh
(And there's no smell of fish)
And we stayed there until it was dark!
We exclaimed in delight
And not in fright.
When we saw how high the slide
For from seeing the view.
We instantly knew
That down we would swiftly glide!
We saw our friends arrive
In a group of five
With hair in ribbons and bows
And the boys each wore a cap
And the smallest one napped.
And the toddler played with his toes.
He pulled off his sandals
And dug his toes in the sand
And took another scoop in his hand.
He held it up to his nose
And a bit for his mouth he chose!
We had steaming red hot dogs on buns
With mustard and relish and such
And water so lovely and cold
That it needed no ice in the cup!
The taste was so yummy
As we filled our tummies
That we hardly had room for it all—
And felt a bit stuffed to our gills
When it was time to play ball.
All too soon the sun was going down
And we knew that we all had to go.
But we will go back and will not lack
For friends to take with us
When back to the park we go!

Every Picture Tells A Story

🔑 Have students illustrate their writing and their descriptions. Get them to **see** with their words!

- 💡 What does the grass look like? Is it short or tall? Bright green or brownish yellow?
- 💡 What about the flowers? Are they in a flower bed? What color are the flowers?
- 💡 Describe the slide. Is the slide heavy plastic or is it shiny metal? Straight or wavy?
- 💡 What do the children look like?
- 💡 How does the hot dog taste?
- 💡 What games did they play?
- 💡 How did it feel to run in the grass?
- 💡 Were their shoes on?

🔑 Have the students work in twos to come up with variations of their park stories. Then, have them start from scratch and write a story selecting:

place, time, activity, number of people, sights, sounds and time of day.

Punctuation Bulletin Board

Put several phrases about a mixture of things on the bulletin board and then big punctuation marks. In order to teach about sentence structure and punctuation usage, let them take turns going to the board and arranging the phrases in a sentence with the correction punctuation. The board can stay up with phrases and words being added daily.

Examples: John is running in a race. John is a big boy. Sue is a girl. Spot is a bad dog. Mom baked cookies. Who sent a box of cookies at the post office? Who loves chocolate, nuts, candy bars, and chips? Who wears a cowboy hat to play? Who sings in the shower? Who loves to bake cakes and pies? Loves to sing and dance?

Try to have several storylines going at once so that they can have the enjoyment of creating fun, silly and mixed up sentences which are technically correct.

Punctu-who?!?

A sentence begins with a capital letter.
(Don't forget, because now you know better!)
And if it merely states a fact,
A period goes at the end
As when you say "Jack is my friend."
A sentence that expresses surprise,
"Hey! They brought us fries!"
Will have an exclamation point
Standing proudly at the end!
Or "Wait! Stop! That's my friend!"
If you have a question to ask,
You don't want a colon or dash,
But a question mark
"When will it be dark?"
Is needed to be at the end.
So remember if a sentence you compose
Such as "There's a fly on my nose."
Keep in mind how you say it
And mentally replay it
And soon the right marks will be there!

Exclamation Mark!

When something is very exciting
Or very forcefully said,
Don't settle for a period,
But use an exclamation point instead!
"Help! Stop! Look! Ouch that hurts!"
See how well an exclamation point works!

The Common Comma

Commas are so funny—
A period with a tail,
Reminds me of a lobster
Or perhaps a big ole whale!
A comma separates things
When listed in a row.
When saying, "I need milk, flour, candy and ice-cream."
Then a comma is the way to go!
It can also be used to separate clauses
At the sight of a comma, your mind pauses.
A comma gives a chance to take a rest,
Letting you enjoy reading at its best!

The Dictionary Bulletin Board

So many students neglect to learn how to utilize a desk copy of the dictionary today because of the availability and ease of using computers for spell check and definitions. Create a double page dictionary display on the board complete with guide words and entry words to give them a taste of using a hand-held, non-electronic, old-fashioned dictionary. One way to create the page, is to scan a copy of it and enlarge it to poster size. Then, print it on a large format printer or copy machine.

The Dictionary

The Dictionary has many uses–
It really is our friend.
It is packed full of knowledge
From beginning (A) to (Z) the end.
In it. I find definitions
Or how to spell a word
And by sounding it out
I can look up words I've only heard.

As you help students develop their technical writing skills, create boards to give them opportunities to develop their creative writing abilities and story telling. Use things that are available in your own home or classroom. Use calendar pages. stationary pages with quotes on them. greeting card sayings and photos. magazine pages and ads to arrange on the board with leading questions to jump start their creative process. Mount the students stories on colored construction paper or cardstock and arrange them next to their inspiration.

You Have a Story

Bulletin boards can have a picture of a different student each week. The other students can take turns interviewing the Student of the Week and writing a news article or story. Make it more interesting by using the computer to create a magazine cover or newspaper mock up for the board. As you change the Student of the Week or Month. have them submit questions ahead of time and then. draw them out of a box or have the class raise their hands and ask the interviewee.

121

🔑 The board can display the student and their achievements from the year. You could have them bring in their soccer shirt or dance shoes.

🔑 List their favorite likes and dislikes. These are some things that can come up during the interviews.

🔑 The students awaiting their turn can make notes of things they want to share with the class when it is their turn to be interviewed.

🔑 Take photos of the board each week and create a special binder of all the students. Have copies made at the end of the year to give to each student to remember their classmates and classroom.

Learning from the Comics

🔑 Keep an eye out on the comic strips for illustrations for different kinds of writing that is fun to read.

🔑 After posting some of the favorite strips for the students to study, have them create their own cast of characters and create a strip of their own. This is a great way to bring in the subject of art.

🔑 Explain to the students the use of the bubbles, various sound effects and the flavor of the strip.

🔑 Research the authors or find collections of their strips to share with the class.

See You in the Funny Papers

Where in the World Are You?

Copy small pieces of maps from different countries and put them on the bulletin board with the above caption. Let the students research on their own or in teams to see who can find the location of the town. If no one is successful, enlarge the area and see if the students can find it with a bit more information available. You can start with easy locations in their own state. Then, as they get better in their research, make it more difficult to find locations.

Learning from History

Display inventors and their inventions. Have students research one of their choice. Write a story about the inventor and how he came to be. Or have students come up with an invention of there own! What would they invent? What would it do? How would it help mankind? What would it look like?

Who Are You?

For a history and a writing board combined, place some facts about a famous historical figure on the board and have students guess who the person is. Leave the person on the board until someone has guessed correctly. Throw in some surprises once in a while and include one of their classmates, a teacher, or the principal.

The Rest of the Story...

Health

Here are some ideas to use to encourage students of various ages to take care of their bodies and minds using good health, hygiene and nutrition. There are many places on the web where you can download the appropriate photos to include with the verses and quotes below. A dental office might provide a chart of the teeth for your board.

Teeth

I always brush my teeth
So very efficiently.
Every night before bedtime.
So my nice smile you can see.

I want my smile to stay
Very pretty and so white.
So, I must remember to brush
Morning, noon and every night!

Brush your teeth
And take good care of them!
For what they say is true-
You must be true to your teeth
So they won't be false to you!

Brush Those Pearly Whites

What Is A Healthy Diet?

Veggies are good for me.
I love the way they look.
And some are tasty foods.
That you don't have to cook!

Fruit and veggies are good for us
And very easy to prepare.
And if you have an apple or orange.
There is enough for you to share.

I love the taste of ice cold milk
And I don't mind a bit of cheese.
I try to avoid using too much salt
And pepper makes me sneeze!

Whole wheat bread is good for me
And I think that it is yummy.
But most of all I love the taste
Of ice cream in my tummy!

Cheese is so very tasty
And yogurt is so fine.
I love my breakfast cereal
And I love tomatoes right off the vine!

Most of us love to have fish and meat.
As well as rice and beans.
Isn't it nice that the food groups
For everyone's preference include something?

Find some pictures from magazines
Of things that keep you healthy.
For a person whose body is well—
Certainly is very wealthy!

Junk Food Junkies

I'm a junk food junkie
And I don't want to be.
Can you tell me
Treats that are
Good for me?

The Pyramid

It's not like the great pyramids in Egypt
And will not bring us wealth
But it is intended to guide us
As we learn to eat for our good health.

🔑 Find a copy of the food pyramid (the most updated version) and post it showing the basic food groups. This would be a good time to explain to the class the seriousness of some food allergies and, especially, if any of the kids in the class have them.

- 💡 Bread, Cereal, Rice, and Pasta Group
- 💡 Vegetable Group
- 💡 Fruit Group
- 💡 Milk, Yogurt, and Cheese Group
- 💡 Meat, Poultry, Fish, Dry Beans, Eggs, and Nuts Group

I'm A Heart Smart Kid!

Why Is Smoking Harmful?

I Won't Smoke!

I will say, "NO" to cigarettes!
And cigars I will decline.
For I want to protect from illness,
These healthy lungs of mine.
If you have seen the photos of lungs that smoke
(Or that belong to folks who do)
The sight of them should be enough
To show that it's not the thing for you!

Just Say No

Some people may ask you
To try something new
And may offer drugs to you.
But turn them down
And turn them in,
For with things such as drugs
You just can't win!

🔑 Research the effects of smoking and share with the class. Younger and younger students are beginning to smoke and drink.

🔑 A small bulletin board can have simply NO NO NO NO NO NO NO NO NO to DRUGS! You might scatter No's of all sizes and colors around the board for effect.

🔑 Share with the class some age appropriate information on the dangers of drug use. What you share will depend upon the age of your class.

🔑 A bulletin board could even include their photos and reasons they have thought of as to why they should say no to drugs.

🔑 EXAMPLE: Photo of Fred with balloon type insert with words "Drugs damage your brain and your ability to think."

🔑 A good way to do bulletin boards with important messages is to create a facsimile of a well known newspaper or magazine. Do the framework, and the headlines and then, use the other collected material as the ads and the articles.

Respect you should be showing for a brain that is still growing

About the Eyes

🔑 Use your favorite ads and periodical covers, etc. to create a variety of bulletin boards. They can be very creative, informative and eye-catching.

🔑 Draw a large diagram of the eye and label each part. Teach the students about the purpose of each part and how to protect and take care of their eyesight.

What Can We Learn From Eyes?

Look around you at the different types of eyes on various animals, mammals and insects. There are also things in inanimate objects such as cameras that we refer to as eyes and also we say the eye of a storm but these are not the same as the wonderful eyes that give us our sight.

Eye See You

We have eyes that allow us to see
I can see you and you can see me.
Other things have eyes but not like ours.
You don't see eyes in trees or flowers.

But puppy dogs and kittens have eyes.
Goldfish have them and so do flies..
They are important and must be
Protected so carefully.

While we don't know
What we would do without them.
Fish deep in dark waters-
Don't even know about them!

We can see our world
Because we also have light.
But would we have eyes to see.
If we had only night?

Seeing Is Believing!

Parts of the Eye

The **eyeball** is the socket and protected by the **lid**.
It has protected you by **blinking**
When something was coming toward your head!
Your **lashes** keep the dirt out
When you are in the wind.
And the **tear ducts** keep it moisturized
(Helping to protect your eyes.)
The **sclera** is the **white part** which is the tough cover.
While the **cornea** is **transparent**, and lets the
Light come shinning through.
So that the world around us
Can be seen by you!

The **iris** is the part that may be brown.
Or green or blue.
The iris has **muscles** attached to it that allows the iris to
Control how much light goes through the pupil for you.
The **pupil** is the black circle in the center
Of the iris. (remember that?) and it lets light enter the eye
So that you see the softball and hit it with the bat!

Between the iris and cornea is the **anterior chamber**.
Filled with a special **transparent fluid** which provides
The eye **oxygen, protein,** and **glucose** to keep it
Healthy so that you can see!
Each part of the **eye** is important to you and me!

continued...

And that's not all! We haven't even mentioned the **lens**
Whose job is to focus light rays on the back of the eyeball.
This **retina** is in the back of the eye
which holds millions of **cells** that are sensitive to light.
The retina takes the light the eye receives and changes it
Into nerve signals so the brain can understand
What the eye is seeing and so we can see it right!

Show Me the Titles!

Creating bulletin boards is such fun and a creative outlet
as far as coming up with fun titles, catchy phrases and
unique designs. But almost anything can be foder for a
bulletin board. Whatever the subject you can do serious
or fun and funky boards.

The Year Begins

Headed Back to School-The board can look like
many converging and diverse streets with cars and
buses and bikes headed toward the school building.
This can be an enlarged photo of your school. You can
have your photo taken in front of the door welcoming
the students back to school or a photo of the entire
staff.

The World's Best Classroom-a Beehive of
Activity... If you can, decorate on the wall or around the
door or even outside in the hallway for the kids to see
as they come into the classroom. Create a hive with the
students as busy bees.

Jumping Into Fifth Grade-The board should include a person jumping, a hand held jump rope. Place around it, things that the students can look forward to learning this year.

Jack Be Nimble-For the youngest students, Jack could be jumping over a candlestick which is sitting on books that have subjects they will learn about.

Refuel For Free-On the bulletin board, a photo of the gas pump and its high prices, and then, a photo of a stack of books and someone reading.

Our School is Cool!-Penguins are so cute and easy to draw. They can be scattered over the board with various sweaters and mufflers, etc. You can use them to introduce the kids and have different names on them or holding books with different subjects on them.

Chill With a Good Book-Penguins again... I love penguins! Could be a single penguin wearing shades and holding a book.

Wanted...Good Students-Create a wanted poster for each student and under the photo put their special abilities or talents.

Want Ads-Look through the newspaper and get ideas to create want ads for specific students or talents. These could be handed out as flyers and have the students find the individual in the class that the ad matches.

Wanted: Seven year old who loves spotted pups and older brothers— Must love math and singing.

Good Citizens in Training-Trains are wonderful and you can be so creative with them. You can use them for fun bulletin boards and learning tools in every subject.

Math Bulletin Board Titles

Math Counts!

Divided We Stand

Do You Speak Math?

The Sum of Our Parts

Things to Do With Math

How Far Can You Count?

Multiplying is Satisfying

Mathematically Speaking

Digits? Integers? Numeral?

How I Used Math This Week

Just a Fraction of Our Skills

Using Math in Our Daily Lives

The World's Largest Numbers

World Famous Mathematicians

How Do You Divide a Pumpkin?

🔑 The boards for these can be as simple as a restful background with mathematic signs and symbols arranged throughout or you can have artwork depicting various activities in our daily lives where math is a necessity.

🔑 The border around the math boards could be colorful addition and subtraction. division and multiplication signs.

🔑 Adding machine tape can be decorated to use as the border around the board.

🔑 Photos could be added to the board from the students. Have them be on the alert for ways that their families use math each day. It could be Dad working on the car. Mom cooking or scrapbooking and cutting mats to exact measurements. Sis sewing and measuring a hemline. Grandma knitting or Grandpa taking his pulse after a workout.

Scintillating Science

We Are Not Alone-Our Solar System

Secrets of Science-Interesting facts on the board

We are Scientists-Draw outlines of students heads on black construction paper and put them on the board.

Surprising Science-Place interesting facts and photos on board.

Don't Let Science (or Math) Puzzle You- Puzzle Pieces with problems on them

Back to the Lab-Board can have all kinds of lab equipment on it and can include simple experiments.

What Our Class Has Discovered-Experiments We've Done... Results We Have Found

We are scientists
As we go about our day
Learning wonderful things
At work, home or play!

Lasting Love of Language

🔑 The bulletin board could have a border of writing instruments, old fashioned or computer era. The actual base of the board could be of a soothing color with the papers matted on various colors. You may even find a gift wrap paper that you like that will go well with your ideas.

Express Yourself-Phrases that we love to use and hear

Eloquently Speaking-Formal writing and writers

Book Your Flight-Book covers of books that take us to far away places

Bards of a Feather-Famous Shakespearean writers and poets

What We Say is What We Get-Add to the board sayings that we use that can be confusing especially to non-Americans or new Americans. Find sayings that are colloquial in nature and collect them from around the country...Pennsylvania Dutch sayings, Southern terms, Bostonian, etc.

Well-Versed-Have the students contribute verses that they have enjoyed and print them out to include on the board. Add to this board, verses that the students write inspired by these verses.

How does one define a teacher? We need more words!

Easing into Essays

Depending on design of the bulletin board various themes could be hidden or included that will give them suggestions for things to write about and share with the class for special assignments or extra credit.

- **January** for the New Year, the board or the border of the board could have Baby New Year holding his hat with little pieces of paper included so that you can take them off the board.

- **February** could have a cheery tree with tiny slips of paper that you can pull out with assignments and different challenges on them.

- **March** winds could be depicted with brightly colored kites each with a tail that has an idea suggested on it.

- **April** could be filled with clouds and raindrops coming down.

- **May** could have a border of flowers just ready to pick.

- **June** could have tiny lady bugs holding suggestions.

- **July** hints could be in the fireworks.

- **August** could be fish swimming in the pool.

- **September** could be school books stacked up.

- **October** could be Fall leaves or pumpkins.

- **November** begs for turkeys and all the fixin's.

- **December** has a million Christmas possibilities.

These could be chosen when some have finished a class assignment early and want something to do for more credit or specific rewards.

Historically Speaking

A border for your History bulletin board could be created with silhouettes of the presidents or pictures of famous documents or historical buildings.

If you don't have room or inclination for the border, then use them sparingly on the base of the board. Use them as a background or embellishments.

Heading Back in Time: Spaceship landing in middle of some historical event.

Time Capsule: Have students add things to the board that would tell people in the future about our lives today.

Time Machine: Time machine landing today in town.

Look Who Was There: Take photos of students and create a bulletin board of historic events placing their photos on the board.

If I Were President: Have students write about what they would do as president of the U.S.A.

If I Were President

If I were elected president
And got to serve our land
In such a very special way
Oh, my, that would be grand!

There are so many things
That I would want to do
But how would I know where to start?
I don't know-do you?

Favorite Elements to Use

Some elements that really lend themselves to creative boards related to most any subject are:

Animals—teddy bears, penguins, puppies, birds, bees, turkeys, fish, frogs, elephants, and whales.

Mechanical—trains, cars, school buses, airplanes, boats, hot air balloons, race cars.

Miscellaneous—You can use baskets, gifts, lights, boulders, pebbles, sign shapes, circles, coins, light bulbs, hands, feet silhouettes, cameras, movie camera, movie lights, stage curtains, spotlights, sharp pencils, etc.

Musical Clefs—notes, paper, harp, piano, drums, cymbals, horns

Nature—trees, pumpkins, Christmas trees, flowers, ocean, seashore, seashells, apples, bananas, leaves, snow, people, birds, hawks, eagles, owls, pigeon, seagulls, fishing

Sports—footballs, basketballs, softballs, baseballs, tennis racket and ball, golf clubs, soccer balls, playing fields, basketball hoops, and even uniforms with hats and shoes

Toys—kites, drums, tops, toy soldiers, balloons on strings

A Board Full of Fun!

How You Can Use Them!

Airplane—Flying High in the Sky to Watch the Clouds Go Passing By... Flying into Math... Flying into Science...

Apples—An Apple a Day... You're the Apple of My Eye... Have students research apples for their nutrition, any myths of their history, their uses and add these to the board. Have them research Johnny Appleseed and his route across the country.

Basket—Basket Full of Wisdom... Bushel of Books... Bushel of Ideas... Basket Cases... (Can be essays of funny stories)

Birds—Look Who's Talking... Papers Not For the Birds... We're Chirping About... And depending on the type of bird, use that in the title like: parrot, macaw, pigeon, seagull, cardinal, sparrow, crow. Something to Crow about... Papers from Smart Gulls and Buoys...

Bee Boards—Buzzing About Doing a Honey of a Job in Ms. Smith's Class... Come into Third Grade and See What the Buzz is About... Sweet Success in Fourth Grade... Look Who's Been Busy as a Bee in Math...

Car—Put math problems along the highway for the students to solve. Have the basic shapes along the highway as well as a school bus. Use titles such as: Driving Along In My Math Mobile... On the Way to Fifth Grade... We Go to School to Learn... Then, list facts that this group will learn.

Christmas Trees—Use trees to encourage students to give to an angel tree drive. Have a large tree on the board and have them add ornaments. If they want to give a gift to a toy drive, they can add the name of the toy they want to donate on the back of the paper ornament. Trees can be created on small boards by using small photos and adding them to the wall in the shape of a tree.

Cool Papers—Chilling With Fifth Grade... Cold Hard Facts of Math... Burr–illiant Book Reports...

Cows—MOO-VING into Math... MOOOre About Science... MOO-ving Stories to Share... Use cows to decorate boards in rustic scenes and use play on words to showcase papers in any subject, especially for language studies. There is a famous artist who creates and paints cows. Look at his work and let students have an art project and paint cows in that way. (Look up Cow Parade in Kansas City on the web.)

Dolphins—Swimming With the Dolphins... What Does a Dolphin Eat? The board can be a big Willy type dolphin taking up most of the board and marine life studies on the board.

Drums—Marching to a Different Drummer... Show pictures of famous people and write about some of their differences. Little Drummer Boy for Christmas Holiday... Listen to the Beat... Drum Roll, Please... For honor roll or top papers.

Elephants—It's a Jungle Out There... Use this as a board to study the countries and habitats of various animals. An elephant may be drawn by the students and may be made as tall as the board and include as much or as little of the elephant as you have space for.

Fish—Fishing for Good Grades... Summer Vacation Fun... Catch a Whopper of a Story... Fish Tales...

Flowers—Bloom Where You Are Planted... Big blooms can be on board to illustrate either science and the way flowers are planted, pollinated, and bloom or as a way to share their writing of their hopes and dreams. Papers can be matted and added to the board among the flowers.

Frogs—Jumping into Math... or English or Science or Jumping into Second Grade... Hoppy You Are Here...

Hot Air Balloons—Decorate the board with brightly colored hot air balloons. Looking for Adventure in Books... Books That Take Us Away... Up, Up and Away With Science... See What All the Hot Air is About...

Kites—Got the World on a String... Sailing Through the Sky Watching the World Go By... March Winds Keep Our Kites Flying High... Use kites as designs for boards about the month of March, weather, etc.

Gifts Wrapped—Birthday Wishes to... A Gift for You From Your Teacher... A Great Book is a Gift... A Smile is a Gift You Give Each Day...

Lights, Camera, Action—Look at Our Star-Studded Fifth Grade Class... Look Who is On Stage... Lights Please!... Your Name in Lights...Top Performances...

Musical...Clefs—You Are Music to My Ears... Notes to You... A Melody of Artistic Style... Use music notes and paper. Musical instruments can be used to create a board for the music department or for other classes as well.

Nature—Post a beautiful scenic view from a calendar on the board and let students write essays, which can then be placed, on the board for English class.

Ocean—Use a scenic ocean view to be the background for the study of the world's oceans and their marine life as well as weather, tides, etc.

Penguin Board—Penguins scattered throughout the board holding either math problems, spelling words, essays, papers to show excellent work, etc. Our Work is Cool... How May I Serve You...

Pumpkins—Thanksgiving, Halloween or Fall boards... In Search of the Perfect Holiday Pumpkin... Have students bring in their pumpkin photos and then, have them tear a pumpkin out of orange construction paper to mat their photos on the bulletin board. Also, add some recipes for making baked pumpkins seeds, pumpkin pie, etc.

Puppy Love—Everyone Loves... This board could be used to showcase essays written about the students animals or something they love.

Race cars—Racing Ahead in Fifth Grade... Race to 2006... Meet You at the Finish Line... The Northside 500... Count laps down to an event.

Sailboat—Sailing into Fourth Grade... Things That Put the Wind in Our Sails... Use sailboats as border around the main board or sailboats throughout the board and information printed on their sales. Students can make sails of various sizes for the board.

Seashore—Sharing Our Shores... What animals live in the sand on the beach or come up to bury eggs in the sand? Write some stories about the seashore.

Seashells—Seashells Tell Tales... Whose House Was This?... Collection of Shells... Show pictures of the shells inhabited by the animals that left them behind.

Sharp pencils—Our Classmates are Sharp!... Pencil This... Sharp pencils placed around the board and papers placed on board to share.

Snow—There's Snow Place Like Fifth Grade!... Pictures of the community in a snowfall. Have students bring in photos of them with their snowmen. etc. Put these on the board and they can use them for inspiration to write a winter essay.

Spring Has Sprung—Spring is in the Air... Spring into Science... Signs of Spring... Show all things having to do with Spring.

Stage Curtains—Presenting Our Cast of First Graders... Curtain Call... A Class Act...

Teddy Bear—Beary Special Papers... Some things "Bear" Repeating... Big Bears, Little Bears, and Teddy Bears... with colorful teddy bears around the board as a border or with one big bear in the corner. Students papers are presented on the rest of the board.

Tops—Spinning Around... Our Class is TOPS!... Our Work is Tops... We're in a Spin About...

Toy Soldiers—We Are Marching to Christmas... Toy soldiers make a cute border around the board and they are great for the center of the board, too. They can be used for Christmas boards or boards about poetry and drama. These are great to use if class is participating in toy drive.

Trees—I Think that I Shall Never See Something as Wonderful as a Tree... Use a beautiful picture of a tree and then, use it to document the scientific and biological aspects of the tree. A good way would be, to enlarge different portions on computer and print them out to place over the original, explaining each part in detail with leaves, trunk, roots, branches, etc.

Turkeys—Thanksgiving boards...from silly "Eat More Beef" to serious "For This We Are Thankful" using the children's hands as the pattern for the turkeys or a turkey body and colorful feathers made and stuck behind the body with students thoughts on each one.

Under the Sea—"Look What I Caught" boards can include anything from country boy sitting on pond bank. with a fishing pole with fish underneath the water line: to aquarium type scene with modern technology.

Other Subjects For Boards

- A Noteworthy Accomplishment
- Scale Down Your Clutter
- Toot Your Horn...Your Best Work
- Take Note of these Coming Events
- Working in Harmony With Our Classmates
- Drum Beats of Success
- Sports Themes-Be a Sport
- What's Your Game Plan?
- Get In the Game of (any sport)
- Sports Figures and Legends
- Our Team
- Hobbies
- Picture This (photography)
- Lights Camera Action
- Stars on Stage

How to Prepare your Bulletin Boards

You can buy especially made paper to cover the boards or use (depending on the subject of the board):

- Tag board or poster board
- Cardboard
- Gift wrap
- Newsprint
- Aluminum foil
- Old cards
- Old newspapers or maps
- Felt or Fabric
- Sheets or curtains

Create Your Own Backgrounds

Print from blown-up photos or artwork or even old wallpaper books.

🔑 You can find a lot of fun things on the discontinued and clearance aisles of the party supplies section at various stores. These can also be used to create fun borders around the outer edges of the boards.

🔑 Don't forget to check out the isles of the super-market and the drugstore for interesting items to use. Sometimes their items will be shipped in colorful or interesting promotional wrappings which they toss out. If you know someone who works there, ask them to please save some of the most unusual items for your class.

Border-riffic and Easy!

Borders might be created from party supplies and crepe paper decorations or created from old game pieces or even puppets or paper dolls. For Winter, you might trace the students hands and have them decorate gloves which you place around the outside in pairs. Student's school photos might also be used or even postcards from their summer vacations.

You can pull interesting pages from old dictionaries and decorate with them or pages from old books or magazines about to be destroyed from the library, etc.

For world events have the students create News Magazine Covers and use them for each topic being featured on the board.

Are you a person who loves to scrapbook? Think of the layout you can create! Picture the bulletin board as a great big scrapbook page and use the same creative imagination to create great boards. You'll be amazed at the ideas that will flow as you Scrap-Board!

The Biggest One

A bulletin board can be
A scrapbook page so easily.
A little bigger than the regular size
But able to hold a nice surprise.
For those who come into the space.
It will cause a smile upon each face.
So decorate your board and have some fun
And as for scrapbooks-
Yours will be the biggest one!

Topics to "Scrap-Board"

- Boards About the Students
- Boards about the Holidays
- Boards about Math
- Boards about History
- Boards about Grammar
- Boards about Reading
- Boards about Science
- Boards about Citizenship
- Boards about Sports and Teamwork
- Board about Our School and Faculty. Staff. etc.
- Boards about Family Trees
- Boards about Animals and Our Pets
- Boards about Careers
- Boards about Our Town and Its Activities
- Boards about Art Today and in History
- All About Me
- Christmas is Magical
- Mathematically Speaking
- The Pilgrims are History Now!

I Could Have Scrap-Boarded All Night!

Puzzling Bulletin Boards

Everyone from the youngest toddler to the graduate student is familiar with puzzles of one kind or another. Save old puzzles and use the pieces to place around the outside edges of the board.

Create large puzzle pieces from tag board or cardstock and use to create various puzzle related boards. Some ideas include:

Math is a Puzzle—Equations, formulas, symbols, rules, etc of math can be placed on puzzle shaped pieces on the board. The problem and the answer can be written on interlocking pieces.

Puzzled by Poetry—Short verses can be written on puzzle pieces or various words that make up a short poem. The students can find the words on the correctly interlocking pieces that will allow them to create a poem.

Finding the Missing Pieces in History— Write names and events or dates or puzzle pieces and scatter them around the board.

Thinking Outside the Box—Create a great big puzzle box on the bulletin board. Fill the box with topics to be studied. Place question marks around the box. Have students go to the box, take out an item, and find unusual facts about it or ways to use it. The items in the box can be changed weekly.

149

101 Pieces of Trivia—Facts that kids will enjoy

Pieces of our World—Print out the states or various countries and let the students lock them together.

Puzzles and Riddles—List favorite puzzles and riddles on the board.

Historical Famous Faces

For each month choose a famous historical face and place a picture or photo where the students can see it. Have them each draw the face and place those portraits on the board.

They can use various mediums for the likenesses from simple pencil to collage and mixed media. being as creative as they like. Have them each explain how and why they made the choices they did.

Famous Fifth Grade Faces

Have the students do self-portraits and write a story about themselves. Take photos of each student and have the class try to match the self-portraits on the board with the photos you took and printed.

Students come and go year by year— Watch them grow!

Famous Modern Faces

🔑 Choose members of Congress, recent presidents, astronauts, or any newsworthy people and have their photos on the board. Place photos of the activities, jobs or events they are associated with.

🔑 By each person's photo, pin a long string and attach the appropriate photos with the string.

What Do We Know About Weather?

🔑 For the youngest students, a board with a bear or duck to dress in the appropriate outfit for the forecasted weather is always fun. To make it more modern and more personal, take photos of the students with various weather props. John with boots and umbrella, Sue with sunglasses and iced drink, etc., and have the students place the proper one on the board to show the weather for the day.

🔑 Sometimes we neglect to teach about the very things that surround us and affect our lives.

🔑 Find the things that are common to your area and photograph them for your classroom. Discuss the things that are most threatening to your area and discuss what to do in case of such emergencies. This board can help you to have your class prepared for emergencies at home and at school.

Rain or Shine— School is Fine!

🔑 **Clouds-**Various types of clouds on the board. These can be drawn or photos.

🔑 **Lightening-**Various types of lightning

🔑 **Tides-**Photos of tides and tidal waves

🔑 **Storms-**Use examples of hurricanes, tornadoes, funnel clouds, water spouts, rain, sleet, snow and hail.

🔑 **Seasons-**How do the seasons affect the weather?

What Do We Do In Case of...???

🔑 Board should show what precautions you take in case of flood, fire, tornado, bad storm, hurricane, etc.

My Community

🔑 Younger students seem especially thrilled to be part of more personalized boards and displays. They love seeing their names and photos on things in the classroom, especially the youngest ones who have just recently learned to read and write their names and the names of their friends.

🔑 There are many ways to include them and so many ways can be found in the simplest things of daily classroom life.

Let's look at some ways to come up with new and creative ideas. Here are some ideas to recognize your community.

Students—Photos of the students can be taken and used on many types of boards...welcome boards for the new year, learning about each other and the community, weather forecasting and changing outfits or props to name a few.

Pets—Photos of pets can be brought to class and used on board about caring for pets, learning responsibilities, safety, guide animals, how to train a dog, our animal friends and for various holidays where animals may be in costume...i.e., Santa hats, and Halloween costumes.

Hats—Students can bring in various hats from home that family members wear and these can be placed on the board or if they are too heavy, photos can be placed on the board to show different occupations.

We Wear Many Hats—The board could show the different jobs that we each do during our lives every day.

Hats of Our Community Heroes—Firemen, EMTs, Policemen, Nurses, Teachers, and our many volunteers, etc.

Fun Hats in Our Neighborhood—Fast food hats, clown headgear, tiaras and cheese-heads, foam hats, etc.

🔑 If you have photos of the students with various "HATTED" members of the community, they can be placed on the board. Students could volunteer to bring in a specific hat and tell about the hero who wears it.

Boots—Use the same type of boards for boots. Fun boots could include cowboys, work, snow, and rain boots. Even drum majorettes, and high-heeled boots!

Uniforms—Same type of board with the people in the community who wear uniforms.

🔑 Perhaps a policeman and fireman would come to speak and allow the students to try on some of their gear and have their photos taken for the board.

🔑 Uniforms of Those Who Serve Our Community- Have the students write papers to put on the board telling about different uniformed forces and how they serve us.

🔑 Our Parents and Family in the Military-A good board to do now because of all of the students who might have one or both parents serving in the armed forces. Each student, may know some family member or friend that is serving.

🔑 The board could have a world map and photo of the student with string attached to the area where their parent or friend is stationed, etc.

🔑 Board could also include a bit about each of the armed services to help students understand more about the military.

When you are in a strange Place and need help, look for A uniform that you trust.

What Is A Uniform?

A uniform is not just fabric and buttons,
Not just a piece of clothing to be discarded,
But a symbol of the honor due a person
Whose dedication should be rewarded.

The fireman wears his uniform with pride
As he protects us from fire and flame.
And it is with awe of his courage
That I speak the fireman's name.

The police officer is so brave
To venture where others fear.
To help protect our families
And all of those we hold dear.

The military members are so brave and dedicated
And they have been sent so far away.
We should keep them in our hearts and prayers
As we remember them each day.

The uniform does not make a hero.
But rather it is the man or woman inside.
Who serves country, city or neighborhood
And does so with dignity and pride.

🔑 Create a Board of Heroes

🔑 Create a Fire Prevention Week Board

🔑 There are Heroes All Around Us

🔑 Who is Your Hero?

What Does A Hero Look Like?

What does a hero look like?
It's really hard to say.
A hero looks like the EMT
Who goes to work each day.

A hero looks like a neighbor
Who is easily within your view.
A hero looks like a policeman
And a hero looks like YOU!

In Gratitude

Our thanks we give to our heroes
Who serve our country each day.
Our heartfelt appreciation we offer
For all they do and say.

Our appreciation is sincere
For we know that we should be.
Offering prayers of gratitude
To those who help keep us free.

They do not all win medals
Or make the evening news at 10.
They serve their country every day
And you call them your friend.

Heroes Are Everywhere-
Thank One Today!

My Dad's Uniform

When my dad goes to work.
He wears a special suit.
He has a shiny badge
And wears some great big boots!

He can drive a special car
And he has a siren, too.
If you need assistance.
My dad can help you.

If you are in trouble.
I hope that you can find,
A wonderful policeman to help you.
Maybe a daddy just like mine!

Grandpa Is a Policeman

My grandpa is a policeman
And he helps people everyday.
If he sees someone who needs help.
Nothing gets in his way.

Mom says he is a hero
And service is his love.
She says the loving heart inside of him
Was created special by God above.

I don't know much about his job
Or what he has to do or see.
I just know how my grandpa is.
When he is next to me!

Hats

Dad wears a hard hat
When he goes to work each day.
He works on a job where objects could fall
As he digs a hole or builds a wall.
Sis wears a funny hat
As she sells fast food each day.
And brother wears a bike helmet
As he peddles along his merry way.
I love to wear a cap
That has my team name on top of it.
And no matter what job you have-
There is a hat to fit!

Boots

Boots are so important
When you have a job to do.
Which demands more protection
Than you get from a shoe.
Cowboys and ranch hands depend on them
To keep their feet protected.
And fashion models wear glitzy ones
So their feet won't feel neglected!

Students

Look at the students around you-
This is your little community.
Let's work hard to keep it happy
And from quarrels keep it free!
We come from different families
And our homes are different, too.
But here at school, it's really cool,
That I feel connected to you!

Various Boards and Displays

The Backpack Board

Other ways to find things that are of interest to students, is to look at the things they carry in their backpacks or purses: Books, CDs, Gameboys, cell phones or beepers, shoes, socks, textbooks, notebooks, notes to friends and whatever else is in there. These things can be used to create boards that will get their attention.

Books

Book covers make great bulletin boards. Choose colorful ones and fill the board with them. Have the students choose their favorite and write a page about it. Place their papers on the board peeking out from inside the book cover.

What Are You Reading? Our Favorite Authors, Best Loved Fictional Heroes, READ TO SUCCEED! What Book Would You Write? How Would You End Your Favorite Book? Favorite Types of Books.

A Book Fell Open

A book fell open and I fell in-
I may not ever come out again!
I rode with cowboys and sailed the sea.
I met people who were different than me.
I saw dinosaurs and kangaroos,
And I wore clown outfits with big floppy shoes.
I went to the moon and came back again
In my wonderful book-I've found a good friend!

Ancestors Bulletin Boards

So many people are really involved in family history, genealogy and research of their roots, now, that a good board could include photos of their ancestors. They could be used then to research that period in history. The girls might enjoy researching the fashions of the era. Also, the photos could provoke interest in the modes of travel at the time, the landscape, the government, the president at the time, and even what the weather was like. Look at major floods, earthquakes, fires or wars being fought.

Ancestors

We inherited some of the traits
That make our families great,
From the ancestors that we never met,
But our genetics won't let our bodies forget!
We may have traits from parents and grandparents
Or great-grandparents and beyond...
Which means that even though I never met them—
Of them I really am quite fond!

Assignment Bulletin Boards

For older students a board can be the place they check for upcoming assignments, grades of previous assignments and due dates for current assignments. For the younger students you could post assignments that they can do for extra credit.

Assignments

These are your assignments
For the coming week
Be sure to make some time
To take a little peek!
The subjects are listed in order
And the books you need to use.
Please take the time to do each one
And your study period–Don't abuse!

Artwork

Describe something such as an elephant and have the students draw it for the board. Don't tell them that it is an elephant until they have completed their drawing. Place the photo that you were describing on the board along with their drawings. You should get some really strange drawing which the students can write stories about and add to the board.

Brain Power

The board can have an outline of the head or of the brain with the different parts identified. Students can make labels to place on the board showing the activities that each part of the brain controls.

Brain Power

You have the power to learn and to do
Whatever it is that appeals to you!
You have the ability to study and learn
The ability to succeed and accolades to earn.
It's all in your head, yes, that is true!
We're speaking brain power–God's gift to you!

Create A Board of the Student's Work

🔑 Make the board look like a movie poster or book cover.

🔑 List the upcoming assignments as Coming Attractions.

The Wise Old Owl

A wise old owl was flying by
And before he found his nest
He gazed upon these papers
On your teacher's desk.

The wise old owl
Was so impressed
That he put them on this wall
So that these great pages
Could be seen by one and all!

Showers and Praise

🔑 Umbrellas can be used to denote Showers and the theme can be used for more than just your April Showers calendar board.

🔑 Showers of Praise for April Days... Showcase perfect papers of students.

🔑 List ways to praise: Great! You Did it! Way to Go! You Reached Your Goal! Awesome!

You are on your Way to the Top!

Safety Patrol

Use board to show how important safety is to your school. Show the crossing guard, the hall monitors, the office staff, the fire drill rules, fire alarms, play ground rules and anything that is connected to their safety at school.

Safety Patrol

I have my badge and my belt
That shows that I'm the one to guide.
The other students to the bus
As soon as they get outside.

Zoo News

Does your town have a zoo? Be sure to include new special arrivals such as baby pandas or any other newborns on a board or display. Let the students discuss the importance of the animals and the care and feeding of the babies.

Zoo

There is an announcement on the TV
About a new arrival...
Everyone at the zoo
Is bent on its survival.
It's a little baby panda
And as cute as it can be.
Let's all go to the zoo,
So everyone can see!

Titles, Lines, and Books! Oh, My!

School and School Bus Boards

🔑 Create the outline of a school building and have photos of the students at the windows.

🔑 Create a big school bus on the board and place photos of the students at bus windows.

Great Inventors and Inventions

Put photos of common everyday items on the board and the names of the inventors to the side. Have the students place the names with the correct invention after doing research.

Black History Month

🔑 Inventions created by black men and women

🔑 Famous black authors, models, politicians or heroes

Noteworthy and Newsworthy

🔑 Have your students or their families been in the newspaper or even in a magazine? List them on the board. Enlarge the newspaper and circle the article about them.

What We Have Learned this Year

(This board can be for one subject or all subjects...)

You might want to list your goals for what you are teaching the students and have the students help you check off the ones they have mastered. Or you can have the students brainstorm about each subject and list what they have learned. Ask them about any preconceived ideas they had about the subject before you covered it in class.

Who Invented Me?

🔑 Fill the board with various inventions and have the students match the name of the inventor with the invention.

What I Would Invent!

🔑 Have students create their own pages for the board of inventions they would like to create.

Where Do We Come From?

🔑 Fill the board with various products and have students match the country or location from which these products come.

About Time

🔑 Depending on the age group, the bulletin board can have clocks which tell about the basics of telling time.

🔑 For older students you can show time in all of the various time zones in the USA or time zones all around the globe.

🔑 Greenwich Mean Time can be displayed and discussed as well as Daylight Savings Time.

🔑 Also mention the International Date Line.

Questions to post with the clocks:

- 💡 How many seconds make a minute?
- 💡 How many minutes in an hour?
- 💡 How many hours in a day?
- 💡 How many days in a week?
- 💡 How many weeks in a month?
- 💡 How many months in a year?
- 💡 How many years in a decade, a score, a century?

About The Calendar

A bulletin board can have plain or fancy calendar pages on it. Students can discuss the importance of the calendar and the origin of the calendar.

Timeline Bulletin Board

Choose a timeline of your choice and use the bulletin board To lay it out. Have various diecuts or photos available for students to place at the correct spot on the dateline.

Boards And What To Do With It..

Look around you for inspiration. For those of you who scrapbook, think of the bulletin board as a giant scrapbook page and create your titles, your images and your embellishments. You can draw inspiration from everything from ABC's to the daily news. Let's pull out various forms of inspiration and create boards.

Look To The Alphabet For Inspiration:

Aa—achievements in sixth grade...apples for the teacher...our best work...ants and their homes...art and history...autumn...our artwork...astronauts...astronomers... airplanes and the Wright Brothers...animal facts...abacas and math...around the world...anchor

Bb—best foot forward...bees and other insects...be the best you can be...believe in yourself...Black History Month... blue ribbon papers...our bright ideas...bushel of great ideas...bushel of good books

Cc—caution...hard work ahead...computers don't bite... cells and our bodies...colonial life and times...cloud types

Dd—designs of nature...dinosaurs...double-digit numbers

Ee—energy from the sun...environment around us... eagles...energize your studies...elections and government...

Ff—fabulous facts about...fundamentals of (learning)... farms and products for our table...firefighters and other heroes...faces of the presidents...world leaders...men in science... women in science...flags of the world...finding rhythm around us...forces of nature...fixing our sights on success...food for thought...found fountains of knowledge fuel for our minds

Gg—getting to know fractions...great presidents...great inventors...great ideas...getting into geography (Grand Canyon)

Hh—helps for learning...helping hands...human body...hats off to our super stars...how we got our flag...history of our nation...holidays...handy facts about...homes around the world...humming along...hear us roar (perfect papers)... hibernating animals...home town heroes...how to (do anything)

Ii—imagine how life will be in 3003...information highway...imagination...incredible journeys...insects

Jj—just for fun...writing...juggling our priorities...just me

Kk—kick it up a notch by going the extra mile for extra credit in math (science. literature)...keep motivated...kindness

Ll—lighting the skies-astronomy and constellations...learn sign language...librarians pick...languages...life in other places

Mm—moving in the right direction...moving on in math...music...microscopic life (veins)...magnets...managing your time with good study habits

Nn—nature...now is the your time to shine...novel ideas

Oo—our bodies-how they work...open up a good book...ocean life...other countries and their culture

Pp—in praise of perfect papers...pledge of allegiance... plant life...proud to be an American (Canadian. French)... proud to be me...pilgrim life...practice makes perfect

Qq—quest for the best...our research papers...quizzes

Rr—reaching for the stars...rainforest...rhythm in music

Ss—striving for excellence...see what we see...story starters...space...solar system...science...speed of sound

Tt—taking stock...what have we learned so far...time to learn about...things that make us smile...toadly awesome facts...talking about-sights. people. words. etc.

Uu—understanding the universe...using a map or compass...using a computer...using our minds...using idioms

Vv—variety in our choices...Veteran's day...Valentine's Day...volcanoes...victorious battles

Ww—watching what we eat...healthy diets...weather reports...where are we...who's who...winners...wacky facts...wise owls...who did it...westward ho...wild things

Xx—"x"tra-special studies...exact measurements

Yy—you are here...historical events as if you are there

Zz—zoological studies...zips and zingers (new vocabulary)

ABC's Just For Me!

More Inspiration

🔑 TV ads can give you some great ideas as well as magazine ads and even ads from internet sites.

🔑 Sports can offer a good way to present various subjects

- 💡 Out of the ballpark papers
- 💡 Skating through the fifth grade
- 💡 Sailing into second grade
- 💡 Dive into math, swim, surf
- 💡 Jump into geometry
- 💡 Riding the waves with math skills
- 💡 Biking, skiing, ballooning, skydiving,
- 💡 Above the clouds...(hot air balloons, blimps, etc)

Hobbies Add Inspiration

🔑 Reading, writing, collecting, quilting, photography

🔑 Stamping, scrapbooking, art, cooking

🔑 Positive and Negative Thoughts About...

🔑 Picture Perfect Papers or Picture This

It Isn't Hard To Be Inspired!

When I'm surrounded
By all the things I love to do,
To feel inspired is not so hard
And I'll bet it's the same for you!
Reading a story I enjoy
Or painting a picture or two,
When all is said and done,
Is an awful lot of fun,
And my creativity comes shining through!

Be Inspired By Movie and Book Titles

- The Great Race in Space
- Miracle On Our Own Street
- Beethoven and His Music
- Under the Sea
- White Christmas in Our Town
- Polar Express
- How the West Was Won
- The Molar Express...Our Teeth

More Miscellaneous Titles for Boards

This can be a very basic board to display papers from your writing workshop or regular classroom assignments.

Blue Ribbon Papers-make or buy blue ribbons

Star-Studded Work-create stars from cardboard and foil

Award Winning Papers-trophies around the paperwork

Praise for Perfect Papers-words scattered around board

Bright Ideas-light bulbs can decorate the board

On Top of the Heap-stack of papers

Here We Are-Each One a Star-stars and students photos

What Makes Us Tick-clocks of various sizes and types

Don't Just Sit There— Write Something!

Animal Planet-Study Of Our Animal Friends

- Discovering our four-legged friends
- Our fine-feathered friends
- Our cold-blooded friends
- Nature's music

Experiments And Projects

What We Did-Photos Of The Project

How We Did It-Description Of The Steps

What We Wrote-Display Of Papers

What Inspired Us-Show Photo Or Drawing Of Inspiration

Then And Now And Future

Put these categories at the top of the board. Decide on a starting date for the "then" category such as the American Revolution or 1776 or even, 1956, and then, find items for all of the following categories:

- **Science-**What was the newest scientific discovery?
- **Politics-**Was there a war? Peace? President?
- **Inventions-**Telephone? Telegraph? Sewing machine?
- **Fiction-**Famous authors? Famous books?
- **Humanities-**What name stands out?
- **Entertainment-**Actors? Singers? Dancers?
- **Industry-**What did we import or export?
- **World leaders-**What leaders were the most powerful? What countries?

Some Board Title Ideas For Upper Grades:

- King of the Jungle
- Pride of our Den
- Fast Track to Success
- Powerful Papers
- Point Counterpoint
- Fact or Fiction?
- Who's Who in the News?
- Define Your Dreams
- Designing Your Future
- Your Path to Success
- Our Heroes
- Race to Space
- Leaders in Our Community
- The Genius Within
- Making History
- Who Will Be the Next President?
- How Do You Make (brownies)?
- Where is (Lowes, KY)?

Nature's Oddities

- Predators and Parasites
- Deserts and Grasslands
- Mountains Ranges of the World
- Famous Explorers
- Plants and Their Parts
- Where Does Silk Come From?
- How Do Spiders Spin Webs?
- Life Cycle of Butterflies
- Our Planet Then and Now
- Animals in the Air and Under the Sea
- Currents and Tides
- Solar Impacts
- Fierce Fighting Animals with Fangs

Health

- Dealing With Diseases
- Healthy Habits
- Learning About the Food Chain
- Why Does Our Skin Do That?
- Layers of our Skin
- How Our Bodies Work
- What We Look Like Inside

Geographical Ideas

- How Do You Get to (the Grand Canyon)...
- Paris Looks Like This...
- Have You Seen France?
- What Products Come From...

Social Issues For Teens

- The Teen Scene
- Mastering the Art of (Writing)
- Communication
- Good Manners
- Introductions
- Social Graces
- Interviews
- Computers
- Keeping Our Minds Healthy
- Say No to Drugs

Music

Musical Gifts
Gift wrapped packages including instruments, etc.

Welcome Bach to School
A welcome board of highlights from Bach's life.

Noteworthy Accomplishments
Put notes around board with photos
of accomplishments of students

Reading Between the Lines
Board will have music papers on it to use
and mats for photos or papers to be displayed.

Compose Yourself
Enjoy the Works of (Mozart)
Use any famous composer or musician.

Different Drummers
People who made a difference
and did things in a new way.

Why We Love Music
Papers written by students about their love of music.

Sing Out!–Students tell what they love about music.

Getting Vocal–Create a board about singing!

Fun-damentals of Music–What makes music fun?

Our Musical Heritage–Background of students.

Composers and Their Lives–Introducing the Next...

The Gift of Music

Miscellaneous Boards

Bragging Rights
Showcasing papers

The Write Stuff
Showing papers from a writing workshop

Our Shining Stars
Photos or papers of exceptional projects

On Our Way to College
College prep class work and research papers

Getting Ready to Get Ready for College
Information on colleges

College Bound
Bulletin and pamphlets about local colleges, etc

Packing Up and Ready to Go
Information about college pre-requisites

Know Yourself
Questions students can answer about themselves

Growth and Exploration
Important things students need to learn

More

- Stand By! (A place for assignments or announcements)
- Our Favorite Things to Study
- Our School Rules
- What's the Scoop?
- Rules and Responsibilities

Interactive Bulletin Boards

A Page a Day

Have a board with a continuing assignment where students post a new page of work on top of the work from the previous day. Such as, writing a continuing story, this is an assignment that will last all month.

Don't Bug Me

Have a computer and a mouse cutout on the board. Let students suggest ways to keep the computer safe from viruses and intruders. For lower grades, an introduction to computers and a fun creation of a computer bug.

Eclipses

Provide space on the board for students to draw examples of the various stages of an eclipse. Look for the dates of these from the past or those in during the school year.

Finding a Meal

Put up photos or drawing of various animals and have students find information on how these animals find nourishment. Include birds, insects, some special plants, and humans.

Fire Safety board

Ask the local fire department for some free handouts and, if possible, have them come with some of their gear so you can take photos of them with the students for the board.

Fuzzy Caterpillar Board

Start the caterpillar by creating the face and a short body. Let the students add to it by adding things they have learned in stages.

Mathopoly

Make a game board on the bulletin board. Students move around the board by answering questions or learning skills. Move as a class or choose teams to compete with daily questions. Correct answers get to move up one space. More difficult, bonus questions get to move more spaces.

Milk and Cookies Board

For lower grades, create a board with big cutouts of milk and cookies. Have them add things that go together, like bacon and eggs, cup and saucer, knife and fork, etc.

Mrs. Smith's Sixth Grade Flower Garden

Let students choose a flower they would like to be. Create that flower to add to the garden. The garden can be used as a first week of school introduction board or to have a place to add winners of a contest or advancement in some learning effort presented to the class.

Music in Each Season

Have photos representing each season on the board and show the various music found in each one that is special to that season. For instance, do you sing the same tunes in the summer as you do in the winter? Are there hymns for holidays such as Thanksgiving? How about patriotic tunes?

Opposites Board

Create a board with opposites. On the board, create a big traffic signal with Red and Green as Stop and Go. Have the students talk about opposites that they use each day in their routine conversations. (Is the soup hot or cold? Is he short or tall? Did I pass or fail?) How would you illustrate these opposites on the board?

Picture This

Create a board with a TV, newspaper or magazine look. Post large headlines with space underneath. Let students take photos of events in their community relevant to the National or World News. Post under the applicable headline.

Safety First

Create a safety patrol board with cutouts of a person or cartoon traffic cop cutout. Let students suggest rules to follow and place them on the board. Include walking, biking, skateboarding, swimming ideas if space allows.

Sing Out

Use song titles to illustrate something you are learning. Have students suggest titles and what they illustrate.

Stone Soup

Read "Stone Soup" and talk to the students about how the village came together to create a soup by each contributing what they had. Draw a big kettle on the board. Ask the students what they love to do that will add to the success of your year. Some may love drawing, writing or storytelling, while others help with math or science, etc. This can be varied to fit any subject or circumstance.

Turkey Feather Board

Students write either questions or facts about Thanksgiving and add to the turkey body to eventually create a very fluffy bird.

Who Said That?

Put famous quotations on the board and have students research the quotes and tell you who said it. For younger students, you might have a stack of printed photos for them to look through to find the right author of the quote.

Real Life Boards

- Diversity In America
- Diversity In The World
- Cultures and People
- Christmas Around the World
- Holidays Around the World
- Around the World in Postcards

Driving

- Driver's Education...Watch Out World!
- Learning the Rules of the Road
- License to Drive

New Driver in the Family

I used to sleep at night
In comfort and in peace
But once my son turned 16,
I knew that that would cease.
Now I watch my son drive off
In the family's car,
And trust that he will listen when
I say, "Please don't go too far!
Obey the traffic laws,
Keep both hands on the wheel."
And I trust that he will drive responsibly–
At least I pray he will!

**HOORAY! I'm licensed to Drive
I did it! I passed the driver's test!**

Miscellaneous Poems Just for Fun

Going through my vast files of poetry, I chose a few for you to read for fun, as stress relievers, to illustrate a bulletin board, share with the PTA or just to give you a giggle. I thought if I enjoyed them, perhaps you would, too!

All Kinds of Animals

We study about animals
In our classroom each day.
We learn about how they look,
But what do animals say?
What does a dog say when he barks,
And what about his howl?
How do I know the thoughts
Of the horned hooty owl?
Does a kitten's purr mean happiness
Or is there a meow that means discontent?
And what about that look she gives
When her back is up and bent?
I don't want to get close at all
To a snake that is hissing.
I know when its tongue is sticking out at me,
It doesn't want to be kissing!
The elephant stands so tall and proud
And has a trumpet sound so loud!
But what does he say when he lifts up that snout?
I'd love to know what he talks about!
From a friendly little pup
To the elephant in the zoo
In their own language, I would love to say,
"Hello, how do you do!"

Downside Up-Upside Down

Who's to say that up is up.
And who determines down is down?
Who do you think would object
If my feet weren't on the ground?

I rather like my downside up
And at times my right side down
But at times of downside up...
Does a smile become a frown??

Snowman Soup

Good friends, good fun, good treats
In sunny or snowy weather–
Share a bit of chocolate
And celebrate being together.

Candy canes and kisses
Are good for anytime.
And I'm so happy to share them
With special friends of mine!

So mix a bit of chocolate drink
And pop in a marshmallow or two.
And soon your snowman soup
Will make you feel warmer through and through!

You must share your snowman soup.
For that's how it was meant to be.
You can't just share with one person.
But pass along the same treat to THREE!

Off To College

Be kind to this college student
As she leaves for school today!
I enjoyed having her close to home
And near us every day!

I know that it may seem silly
To mourn the passing of the years.
And to miss someone as they go off to school...
And to shed these motherly tears.

After all. we raised her for this day...
Prepared her from infancy on
To be self-sufficient. confident
Reliable and strong!

Her empty room is hard to face
As is the empty chair.
The bathroom's always free now...
No teenager drying her hair!

I cried as I watched her drive away.
Those tears I still feel on my face.
Each time I find comfort in remembering
The warmth and strength of her embrace!

God bless my grownup child
I give her Lord to You.
And ask that You watch over her
As only You can do.

And heal this mother's heart. Dear Lord.
That hurts so very much.
And when I get too anxious. Lord.
Please let me feel Your touch!

We'll Be Friends Forever

We'll be friends forever.
I knew it from the start
For there was a special feeling
That I felt within my heart.

Whether miles separate us
Or we are close together.
Whether the days are sunny
Or we have stormy weather.

Trials may come to test us.
But our friendship will stay strong.
For there is a friend-shaped spot
In my heart where only you belong.

Friends

In my gallery of friends.
Each of you come into view.
Making me feel fortunate
To have friends like you.

Though we go our separate ways
And eventually all of us will part.
Memories of our happy times as
Classmates will linger in each heart.

There's No Friend Like a School-friend!

Friendship

Friendship knows no difference of age
Nor race, religion or creed.
Friendship forms a special bond
That is all friends ever need.

Friendship is more beautiful
Than the most fragile flower
That in my garden doth bloom,
And each tiny petal smiles a dainty smile
When a dear friend enters the room.

We Are So Proud Of You

You are ready now for a new adventure
And a new era in your life has begun.
Move forward in your usual confident way,
And enjoy the challenge and the fun.

You have strength and character
And your spirit is gentle and sweet.
This is a winning combination,
And you are wonderfully unique.

Stand firm always in your convictions
And continue to be true to who you are,
And know your parents will always stand beside you,
And in life you will go far.

We are so proud of who you are
And who you will yet be,
And congratulate you on your graduation,
And the best is yet to come, you'll see!

What Kind of Happy Are You?

What kind of happy are you?
Are you happy through and through?
Do you enjoy life and love
And everything you do?

What kind of happy are you?
Are you a giddy one?
Do you laugh and joke and jest
And create lots of fun?

What kind of happy are you?
Are you happy once in a while?
Does it take a lot of effort
To make you even smile?

What kind of happy are you?
Are you happy every day?
Do you take joy in your life
And what you do and say?

I pray that you are happy
And that you smile a lot.
I hope you love to laugh out loud
And appreciate what you've got!

Oh. please. be happy
And in all that you do.
Try to help other people
To be happy too!

For joy is contagious—
Just watch and you'll see!
You've been infected now
By this note from me!!

Joy In Little Things

I love to see the joy and laughter
That is found in little things
I love the love and happiness
That childish joys bring!

Oh, to find joy in a sunbeam
Or in a bumblebee-
To see beauty in a blade of grass
As only a child can see.

What happy memories
Are stirred within my heart,
When I watch happy laughing children
Playing in the park!

Black and Blue

It's the strangest thing
That ever I've seen-
I woke up this morning
And I was green!

I was black and blue
And purple, too,
And my Mommy said,
"Oh, look at you!"

She said that bruises
Always go away
And I won't always look this way
But for all the days in between...
It won't be easy being GREEN!

I Love Worms

Mom doesn't understand
My love for bugs and worms.
Whenever I bring home a "friend."
My mom shudders and squirms!

Worms are such wonderful pets
That never run away
You find them a nice pail of earth
And there the worms will stay!

A butterfly will fly away
And has to be out and free.
But when I find a big 'ole worm.
He has to stay with me!

I put them in my pockets
And take them around with me.
To show them all the places.
I think a worm would like to see!

I'd like to show the worms my room
And have them sleep me
But as for now. I'm sad to say.
My mom doesn't agree!

A worm is a wiggly squiggly friend. It looks the same from end to end.

Too Much Stuff

Some folks say they don't have enough
Of all the very interesting stuff
That is everywhere to be found–
Stuff that makes the world go around.

But I have boxes under my bed
And bags in pigeon holes overhead.
And stuff stacked up in the hall.
Over which a person could fall.

It looked so much better without a doubt.
When I took a day to clean it out.
I bundled stuff up and gave it away.
So that my room so neat could stay.

But then. I went back to the store.
And before I knew it
I had bought some more
....Stuff!

Farewell to Freddy Frog

A Fond Farewell to Freddy.
We are so sad to see you go.
But wild things should be set free.
My mommy told me so!

Forgive me Freddie if I cry.
But I'm too young to see–
Exactly why my favorite frog
Would prefer to be set free!

Pet with a Fetish

My pet cat has such a fetish–
He is irrationally attached to shoes!
The attempts I've made to cure him
Of his pre-occupation and propensity,
And tactfully assure him of my intent,
Have ended in defeat for me!
So I sit here and I journal,
Feeling really quite maternal,
Putting my distaste for his obsession from my mind,
And when he attacks his prey,
No matter on whose feet are they,
I just turn my head and look away.
He does not mean any harm or vindictiveness–
He isn't even sick...I guess...
He just has this partiality to shoes,
And it doesn't really matter whose...
Big shoes or small shoes,
Ballet or ball shoes,
He loves them all so equally
That it really is quite humorous to see,
And considers each visitor at our door
With equal opportunity,
He will run up and grab you
And his paws will try to nab you
And around your shoes he will be purring,
No matter how much you are hurrying,
So if you come to visit me,
You might want to know–
There is nothing I can do
If you insist on wearing a shoe.

Teen Room-Enter At Own Risk

There is a sign upon my door.
My mom put it there.
"Enter room at your own risk"
And I don't think it's fair!

I may be a bit untidy
And scatter things a bit.
But I have to try on lots of clothes
To see if they will fit.

And since I'm in a hurry,
Once the trying on is done.
I don't have time to put them back...
I'm off to have some fun!

And when I rush off to school,
I have to leave home in a hurry...
So I don't have time to put things up,
With tidiness I don't worry!

The sign fell off and landed in my room
For it's no longer on my door
And now I cannot find it...
It's somewhere among
...the clothes upon my floor!

**Please be careful
where you sit
I am still missing
my favorite pet...**

Teenagers!

Mom doesn't understand them
And Dad doesn't treat them right.
Both parents should allow them
To stay out later at night.
Parents expect them to be neat and
Teachers expect them to be on time.
Policemen expect them to obey the speed laws
Or else they must pay a fine.
The community wants them to be good citizens
As they do their own teenage thing.
And the family wants to be made proud of them
As they enjoy the exuberance teenagers bring.

Spare Parts

I started to build something
And was using a little kit.
I had lots of stuff left over
Because it wouldn't fit.
The end product loved very cool
And I was quite impressed.
But when it didn't work.
My surplus part I confessed.
Little bits of this and that
And wire and electronic stuff
In the little box
Didn't seem like much...
But evidently each part was important
And was needed just the same.
And the fact my creation didn't work-
Had only me to blame...

About the Author
Thena Smith

Thena was born in a tiny farming community in Western Kentucky where she remained until she married her college sweetheart in 1965. For the last 20 years she has lived in Coronado, California with her husband, Ron and her daughter, Melissa. Thena remembers writing her first poem at the age of 7 for a class Christmas project. Her mom sent it to the local newspaper and it was published. For many years, she wrote, but failed to save her writings. Finally, encouraged by a friend to save her work, she along with friends, presented a collage of poetry and music that was televised on a local cable station. She also co-wrote a children's musical that was presented locally. Thena has always been a scrapper. And, as the hobby began to catch on, she began to share verses with others. A local on the scrapbooking message boards, Thena has written hundreds of poems to share with her many friends.

More of Thena's writings can be found in her two best selling books, "Where's Thena? I need a poem about..." and "Whispers." Can't get enough?? Watch for more of Thena's works to come at www.BluegrassPublishing.com.

Note from Thena: What a surprise when Linda found my website and contacted me about using some of my poetry in her books. I was even more amazed to find out that she lived in Mayfield, Kentucky, a few miles from Lowes, Ky, where I was born and raised. Isn't it funny that I had to move to California to meet her and she moved from California to Kentucky and ultimately met me. Amazing what a small world exists when God has a plan. Since our first lovely chat via e-mail, we are enjoying a blossoming friendship.

Our Favorite Sites

🔅 Be sure to visit the websites of all of our contributing writers. You can find a link to more of their sites on our website at: www.BluegrassPublishing.com.

🔅 Our favorite place for fonts is www.LetteringDelights.com. Doug and his company have the greatest selection of fun, funky and fabulous fonts for all your scrapbooking and crafting needs and wants. Be sure to tell them we said, "Hello."

🔅 For the best in rubberstamps and related products, be sure to visit Posh Impressions, the website of Dee and Warren Gruenig. They are wonderful people and have lots of info and products available. Their website is: www.PoshImpressions.com. We love them!

🔅 This is one of our favorite sites. At Cottage Arts make your memories into lasting works of art with digital scrapbooking ideas and products. You will be inspired! www.CottageArts.net

🔅 Need a website created? Visit Holly VanDyne our great webdesigner. She is a joy to work with and will do all she can to help you develop the site that fits your needs. www.ScrapbookInsights.com.

Our Best Sellers!

We have the <u>Largest</u> <u>Collection</u> of poems & quotes
for scrapbookers and cardmakers ever created!

The Ultimate Guide to the Perfect Word

(Our biggest seller—over 200,000 copies sold!)
Linda LaTourelle

The Ultimate Guide to Celebrating Kids I

(birth through preschool-384 pages)
Linda LaTourelle

Introducing the first book in our new
"Perfect Words Worth Repeating" series...

LoveLines

(artistic quotes to be used time and again)
Linda LaTourelle

Where's Thena? I need a poem about...

(insightful & witty poems)
Thena Smith

Whispers

(passionate poetry & words of love)
Thena Smith

Be sure to watch for all of our books
on Shop At Home Network!
More Surprises
Coming Soon!

New Books

Now Available

The Ultimate Guide to Celebrating Kids II

(All New—Grade School Age–384 pages)

Linda LaTourelle

The Ultimate Guide to the Perfect Card (2nd. Ed.)

(Revised edition—now 384 pages)

Linda LaTourelle & CC Milam

Board Smartz

(learning tips and bulletin board quips)

Thena Smith

Taste of Paste

(poems for the classroom of all ages)

Thena Smith

What Can I Say?

(words with an artistic flair!)

WendiSue

Coming Attractions

Season's Greetings

Linda LaTourelle

C is for Christmas

(poetry for the season)

Thena Smith

The End?

No Way—We hope that
Board Smartz
will inspire you
to create boards
that will educate
and delight
your students
for years to come.

Other Board Ideas

Other Board Ideas

For more inspiration visit our website:

Bluegrass PUBLISHING

w w w . t h e u l t i m a t e w o r d . c o m
2 7 0 · 2 5 1 · 3 6 0 0

BLUEGRASS PUBLISHING, INC.

ORDER FORM

NAME	DATE

ADDRESS

CITY/STATE

CREDIT CARD #	EXP. DATE

PHONE ( ) —	

E-MAIL

QTY	TITLE	EACH	TOTAL
	The Ultimate Guide to the Perfect Word BY LINDA LATOURELLE · OUR BIGGEST SELLER	$19.95	
	The Ultimate Guide to the Perfect Card BY LINDA LATOURELLE · NEW/BIGGER-384 PG	$19.95	
	The Ultimate Guide to Celebrating Kids I BY LINDA LATOURELLE · BIRTH TO PRESCHOOL	$19.95	
	The Ultimate Guide to Celebrating Kids II BY LINDA LATOURELLE · NEW/GRADE SCHOOL	$19.95	
	LoveLines—Beautifully designed quotes BY LINDA LATOURELLE · NEW/COPY & USE	$12.95	
	Taste of Paste: Poems for the Classroom BY THENA SMITH	$14.95	
	Board Smartz: Bulletin Board Tips BY THENA SMITH	$14.95	
	Where's Thena? I need a poem about... BY THENA SMITH	$19.95	
	Whispers: Passionate Poetry BY THENA SMITH	$12.95	
	What Can I Say?: Words With Artistic Flair BY WENDISUE	$12.95	

SEND ORDER TO:

BLUEGRASS PUBLISHING, INC.

(270) 251-3600
PO BOX 634
MAYFIELD, KY 42066
FAX (270) 251-3603

WWW.BLUEGRASSPUBLISHING.COM

6% TAX KENTUCKY	
$2.95 Per Book	S/H Disc. Given on 3 or more
TOTAL AMOUNT	
$	

Thank You

For Your Order

Give a friend
the gift of words
with our ultimate line of books

www.theultimateword.com
270 · 251 · 3600